Hayley Trim is a solicitor with 16 years of experience in family law. From working in London on ultra high net worth and complex international cases to providing technical legal support, information and training to a large national family law team, she has seen cases of many shapes and sizes from the length and breadth of the country. A self-confessed family law geek, she has lectured on the subject of inherited wealth on divorce and has a particular interest in pre- and post-nuptial agreements. Alongside advocating technical legal excellence, Hayley is also a trained mediator and seeks pragmatic and commercial solutions for her clients.

# A Practical Guide to Inherited Wealth on Divorce

# A Practical Guide to Inherited Wealth on Divorce

Hayley Trim
Solicitor
MA (Cantab)

Law Brief Publishing

© Hayley Trim

All rights reserved. No part of this publication may be reproduced, stored in a retrieval system, or transmitted, in any form or by any means, electronic, mechanical, photocopying, recording or otherwise, without the prior permission of the publisher.

Excerpts from judgments and statutes are Crown copyright. Any Crown Copyright material is reproduced with the permission of the Controller of OPSI and the Queen's Printer for Scotland. Some quotations may be licensed under the terms of the Open Government Licence (http://www.nationalarchives.gov.uk/doc/open-government-licence/version/3).

Cover image © iStockphoto.com/vandervelden

The information in this book was believed to be correct at the time of writing. All content is for information purposes only and is not intended as legal advice. No liability is accepted by either the publisher or author for any errors or omissions (whether negligent or not) that it may contain. Professional advice should always be obtained before applying any information to particular circumstances.

Published 2021 by Law Brief Publishing, an imprint of Law Brief Publishing Ltd
30 The Parks
Minehead
Somerset
TA24 8BT

www.lawbriefpublishing.com

Paperback: 978-1-912687-87-9

# PREFACE

The impact and importance of inherited wealth is increasing. It has become trite that that older generations hold a greater proportion of wealth than those born after them. Millennials and the younger generations are finding it harder to get on the housing ladder than their parents and grandparents, have not had the benefit of free university education and are far less likely to enjoy generous pensions. They are more liable to rely on inheritances and gifts from their financially comfortable older relatives.

Recent research shows that inheritances are likely to become considerably larger, not just in absolute terms, but also relative to lifetime employment income.[1] Consequently inherited property will be an increasingly significant factor when relationships break down and property is divided up.

In England and Wales we have a discretionary approach to financial remedies on divorce[2] which aims to achieve a fair outcome taking into account all of the circumstances of the case. However as has been said many times, fairness, like beauty, is in the eye of the beholder and it cannot be assumed that every mind, whether judge, practitioner, academic or lay client, will agree that a particular result is indeed fair. This is perhaps exemplified by cases involving inherited assets, the value of which, together with the emotion which regularly accompanies them, often supported by a weight of family opinion, has a tendency to drive litigation.

Consideration has been given to statutory reform to introduce greater predictability, but when the Law Commission came to consider the treatment of non-matrimonial assets as part of its consultation on

---

1  https://ifs.org.uk/publications/14954
2  Please note that references to 'divorce' throughout this book also apply to dissolution of civil partnerships, and references to 'marriage' apply equally to civil partnerships, unless otherwise stated.

Matrimonial Property, Needs and Agreements in 2014[3] it did not make any recommendations, concluding that it would be too controversial in view of the differing opinions on the subject. Consequently it indicated that couples looking for certainty should enter a nuptial agreement and focused its attention on that subject.

Since there is no specific statutory direction for how inherited wealth should be treated, we must look to the various decisions of the courts and the judicial guidance given in them.

In considering the considerable body of case law it is important to keep in mind these words of Lord Nicholls:

> *"Fairness is an elusive concept. It is an instinctive response to a given set of facts. Ultimately it is grounded in social and moral values. These values, or attitudes, can be stated. But they cannot be justified, or refuted, by any objective process of logical reasoning. Moreover, they change from one generation to the next. It is not surprising, therefore, that in the present context there can be different views on the requirements of fairness in any particular case."*[4]

This book considers the developments since the turn of the millennium and assesses how the law currently stands (25 February 2021) on this increasingly prevalent and important topic.

Hayley Trim<br>
February 2021

---

3 Law Commission's Consultation Paper No 343, Matrimonial Property, Needs and Agreements (26 February 2014)
4 *Miller v Miller and McFarlane v McFarlane* [2006] UKHL 24 para 4

# TABLE OF CASES

| Case | Page |
| --- | --- |
| Michael v Michael [1986] 2 FLR 389 | 87 |
| MT v MT [1992] 1 FLR 362 | 88 |
| H v H [1993] 2 FLR 335 | 86 |
| White v White [2000] UKHL 54 | 1, 7-12, 13, 21, 47, 50, 91, 96 |
| Cowan v Cowan [2001] EWCA Civ 679 | 12 |
| Norris v Norris [2002] EWHC 2996 (Fam) | 12 |
| Figgins v Figgins [2002] Fam CA 688 | 13 |
| GW v RW (Financial Provision: Departure from Equality) [2003] EWHC 611 (Fam) | 13 |
| P v P [2004] EWHC 1364 (Fam) | 21, 22 |
| Rossi v Rossi [2006] EWHC 1482 (fam) | 16, 50, 59 |
| Miller v Miller and McFarlane v McFarlane [2006] UKHL 24 | 4, 13-15, 16, 21, 30, 32, 34, 35, 37, 42, 44, 47, 48, 49, 62, 70, 96, 101 |
| NA v MA [2006] EWHC 2900 (FAM) | 31, 34, 54, 77, 78 |
| Charman v Charman (No 4) [2007] EWCA Civ 503 | 28, 29, 42, 44, 81 |
| Vaughan v Vaughan [2007] EWCA Civ 1085 | 33, 35 |

| | |
|---|---|
| C v C [2007] EWHC 2033 (fam) | 62, 78 |
| H v H (Financial Provision) [2009] EWHC 494 (Fam) | 49 |
| C v C (ancillary relief trust fund) [2009] EWHC 1491 (Fam) | 87 |
| Robson v Robson [2010] EWCA Civ 1171 | 17, 19, 23-26, 27, 31, 37, 53, 54, 63, 78, 101 |
| Radmacher (formerly Granatino) v Granatino [2010] UKSC 42 | 95, 97, 98, 99 |
| FZ v SZ and others (Ancillary Relief: Conduct: Valuations) [2010] EWHC 1630 (Fam) | 57 |
| Jones v Jones [2011] EWCA Civ 41 | 16, 45, 53, 58, 59, 60, 61, 63, 64, 65, 67, 73, 77, 78, 101 |
| K v L [2011] EWCA Civ 550 | 29, 30, 31, 33, 34, 35, 41, 42, 47-48, 54, 77, 78, 81 |
| N v F [2011] EWHC 586 (Fam) | 43, 50, 51, 57, 60, 61, 69, 78 |
| Whaley v Whaley [2011] EWCA Civ 617 | 28 |
| J v J (Financial Orders: Wife's Long-term Needs) [2011] EWHC 1010 (Fam) | 44, 61, 78 |
| GS v L [2011] EWHC 1759 (Fam) | 38, 78 |
| S v AG [2011] EWHC 2637 (Fam) | 35, 50 |

| | |
|---|---|
| AR v AR [2011] EWHC 2717 (Fam) | 38, 39, 42, 78 |
| Kremen v Agrest (No.11) (Financial Remedy: Non-Disclosure: Post-Nuptial Agreement) [2012] EWHC 45 (Fam) | 97 |
| F v F (Financial Remedies: Premarital Wealth) [2012] EWHC 438 (Fam) | 92 |
| Y v Y [2012] EWHC 2063 (Fam) | 26, 39, 79 |
| AC v DC [2012] EWHC 2420 (Fam) | 51 |
| Luckwell v Limata [2014] EWHC 502 (Fam) | 99 |
| JL v SL (Financial Orders: Property inherited during marriage) [2014] EWHC 3658 (Fam) | 47, 51, |
| JL v SL (No 2) (Financial remedies: rehearing: non-matrimonial property) [2015] EWHC 360 (Fam) | 43, 47, 51, 57, 58 |
| Critchell v Critchell [2015] EWCA Civ 436 | 89 |
| WW v HW [2015] EWHC 1844 (fam) | 96, 97 |
| Scatliffe v Scatliffe [2016] UKPC 36 | 43 |
| Robertson v Robertson [2016] EWHC 613 (Fam) | 64, 73, 74, 79 |
| Christoforou v Christoforou [2016] EWHC 2988 (Fam) | 68, 69 |
| WM v HM (Financial Remedies: Sharing Principle: Special Contribution) [2017] EWFC 25 | 70, 73 |
| Work v Gray [2017] EWCA Civ 270 | 81 |

| | |
|---|---|
| Sharp v Sharp [2017] EWCA Civ 408 | 48 |
| Hart v Hart [2017] EWCA Civ 1306 | 43, 45, 60, 61, 65-68, 69, 70, 71, 74, 79, 83, 101, 103 |
| Alireza v Radwan [2017] EWCA Civ 1545 | 87 |
| Her Royal Highness Tessy Princess of Luxembourg, Princess of Nassau and Princess of Bourbon-Parma v His Royal Highness Louis Xavier Marie Guillaume Prince of Luxembourg, Prince of Nassau and Prince of Bourbon-Parma [2018] EWFC 77 | 86 |
| Waggott v Waggott [2018] EWCA Civ 727 | 92 |
| Versteegh v Versteegh [2018] EWCA Civ 1050 | 72, 79 |
| Brack v Brack [2018] EWCA Civ 2862 | 98 |
| Martin v Martin [2018] EWCA Civ 2866 | 70, 71, 73, 74, 79, 82 |
| Ipekci v McConnell [2019] EWFC 19 | 97, 98, 99 |
| XW v XH [2019] EWCA Civ 2262 | 72, 79, 82, 101 |
| WX v HX (Treatment of Matrimonial and Non-Matrimonial Property) [2021] EWHC 241 (Fam) | 52, 74, 75, 101 |

# CONTENTS

*Preface*

*Table of Cases*

| Chapter One | Introduction | 1 |
|---|---|---|
| | – What is Inherited Wealth | 1 |
| | – Non-Matrimonial Property | 2 |
| | – Statutory Provisions | 3 |
| | – The Future? | 5 |
| Chapter Two | Case Law History and Development | 7 |
| | – White v White | 7 |
| | – Their Lordships' Observations on Inherited Wealth | 9 |
| | – Cases After White | 12 |
| | – Miller v Miller; McFarlane v McFarlane | 13 |
| | – Guidance After Miller | 16 |
| Chapter Three | Nature of the Property | 21 |
| | – Farms and Estates | 21 |
| | – Antiques | 26 |
| | – Trusts | 27 |
| | – Shares and Investments | 29 |
| | – Business Assets | 31 |
| | – The Family Home | 31 |
| Chapter Four | Application of Needs and Sharing Principles | 37 |
| | – Needs | 37 |
| | – Sharing | 42 |
| | – Which Comes First and Which Prevails – Needs or Sharing? | 43 |
| Chapter Five | Other Relevant Factors | 47 |
| | – Time | 47 |
| | – Length of the Marriage | 48 |
| | – Mingling and Treatment of Assets | 49 |
| | – Lifestyle | 53 |

| Chapter Six | Valuing the Matrimonial Element of Inherited Property | 55 |
|---|---|---|
| | – The Formulaic/Mathematical Approach | 57 |
| | – The Impressionistic/Discretionary Approach | 61 |
| | – Hart v Hart | 65 |
| | – Evidence of Non-Matrimonial Property | 68 |
| | – Treatment of Valuation Evidence | 70 |
| Chapter Seven | Departing From Equality – What Is Fairness? | 77 |
| Chapter Eight | Special Contribution | 81 |
| Chapter Nine | Future Inheritances | 85 |
| | – The Usual Approach | 85 |
| | – Forced Heirship | 87 |
| | – Adjournment | 88 |
| Chapter Ten | Inheritance as a Barder Event | 89 |
| Chapter Eleven | Passing Assets On | 91 |
| | – Will the Court Allow Provision for it in an Award? | 91 |
| | – Lifetime Gifts During the Marriage | 92 |
| Chapter Twelve | Protecting Inherited Assets –Nuptial Agreements | 95 |
| | – Needs | 97 |
| | – Meeting the Criteria | 98 |
| Chapter Thirteen | The Present; and Practical Considerations | 101 |

# CHAPTER ONE
# INTRODUCTION

### What is Inherited Wealth?

What is meant by 'inherited wealth' is assets or resources that are passed on to a recipient upon the death or contemplated death of the owner. Typically this will be from one family member to another – wealth passed from one generation to the next – but that need not be the case. In the context of divorce and the division of assets and for the purposes of this book it will be appropriate to include wealth that has been passed to one party to a marriage by a living individual, since it is not uncommon for inheritance arrangements to commence during the donor's lifetime whether for tax planning or other reasons.

In *White v White*[1] Lord Nicholls referred to "*property acquired during the marriage by one spouse by gift or succession or as a beneficiary under a trust. For convenience I will refer to such property as inherited property.*"

The assets that are inherited could essentially be anything, and although we refer to 'inherited wealth' for convenience, that is not to restrict our consideration to 'wealthy' people.

The inheritance or gift may have been received before or during the marriage, or indeed after separation. We will examine different types of asset and the value, source and circumstances of the inheritance and the impact that such factors may have in due course.

One of the features of inherited wealth in the divorce context is that it is from a source external to the marriage which is personal to the recipient as an individual and, at least at the point of receipt, does not generally include monies earned or accrued by virtue of the recipient's endeavours. Therefore it will often fall to be considered as a form of *non-matrimonial property* and the same principles will often apply.

---

[1] *White v White* [2000] UKHL 54

## Non-Matrimonial Property

Non-matrimonial property is not defined in statute. The concept is a creature of case law and will be considered in further detail during the course of this book. A very broad summary is to say that non-matrimonial property comprises assets brought into the marriage or received by way of gift or inheritance by one party to the marriage, together with passive growth on such assets. Or one might look at the flip side of the coin and consider what is matrimonial property or the 'marital acquest'; property that has been acquired during the marriage by virtue of the parties' common endeavour, and which will usually include the matrimonial home and contents, plus assets acquired for the use and benefit of the family. Non-matrimonial property may become matrimonial over time further to 'mingling' or other treatment. It's immediately clear that there are grey areas, but while definitive answers may be desirable for many, it seems they have not been achievable.

The executive summary of the Law Commission's Consultation Paper on Matrimonial Property, Needs and Agreements[2] (which, as its name suggests, had proposed to report on the question of matrimonial/non-matrimonial property) records that:

> *"At the outset of our examination of non-matrimonial property we felt that the courts' practice of not sharing pre-acquired, gifted and inherited property might usefully be captured in the form of statutory rules. We also felt that statute should address the sort of issues that are likely to arise in the context of such property, for example when it is sold and replaced, or grows as a result of the investment of either party. These are issues to which the courts have not yet been able to provide clear answers."*

However they decided against making recommendations in respect of non-matrimonial property:

> *"…Although we would have liked to recommend statutory provisions to address those situations in which the case law has not yet provided*

---

[2] Law Commission's Consultation Paper No 343, Matrimonial Property, Needs and Agreements (26 February 2014) para 1.24 – 1.25

*clear answers, consultation responses have demonstrated that such provisions would be unacceptably controversial."*

Therefore there is nothing in statute to indicate that inherited wealth specifically, or indeed non-matrimonial property, should be treated in a particular way.

**Statutory Provisions**

The Matrimonial Causes Act 1973 (MCA) s25 provides that the court's duty in deciding how to exercise its powers is to have regard to all the circumstances of the case, first consideration being given to the welfare of any minor child of the family. The courts have repeatedly confirmed that the existence of inherited wealth will be one of the circumstances of the case which the court will take into account.

s. 25(2) MCA sets out the factors that the court must consider when deciding what financial remedy orders to make and a number of these are clearly relevant to the treatment of inherited wealth:

(a) **The income, earning capacity, property and other financial resources that each party has or is likely to have in the foreseeable future.**

Inherited assets will be resources available to the parties in terms of the computation stage of the financial remedy process. Their inherited nature doesn't take them out of consideration at least in assessing the extent and value of the available resources. How they are valued and then treated subsequently is considered in detail in due course. Note that resources not yet available but which are likely to be in the foreseeable future will also be taken into account. This will potentially apply to prospective inheritances depending on the circumstances.

(b) **The financial needs, obligations and responsibilities that each party has now or is likely to have in the foreseeable future.**

In the majority of cases, where the available assets do not exceed the parties' needs to a significant extent, those needs will be the determining factor in the division of the assets, even where these have been inherited in whole or in part . In broad terms, if needs require it then the court will have recourse to inherited assets in deciding the overall division; as we will see most cases begin and end here[3]. The interpretation of needs will be further considered.

### (c) The standard of living enjoyed before the breakdown of the marriage.

This is a very important factor as we'll examine in due course. If the inherited wealth has provided for the family during the marriage and kept them in a certain lifestyle, rather than being kept separate and apart, that may justify different treatment. The marital standard of living will also inform needs.

### (d) The age of each party and the duration of the marriage; and

### (e) Any mental or physical disability of either party.

These factors feed into the needs of the parties and the form of and the duration for which financial provision will be required and can be afforded. As with lifestyle, the question of how long inherited assets have been enjoyed within the marriage will be relevant to assessing how they should be treated. Over the course of a long marriage the source of the assets may lose its importance, and there is a greater likelihood that inherited assets will have been mingled with matrimonial assets.

### (f) The contributions which each of the parties has made or is likely in the foreseeable future to make to the welfare of the family, including any contribution by looking after the home or caring for the family.

Assets inherited by one party will usually be a contribution they have made, being from a source external to the marriage. Depending on the circumstances it may be that the inherited assets represent an *unmatched* contribution by one party. Where there are children, one or both parties will likely continue to make a contribution to the welfare of the family and this will be weighed in the balance; the courts are alive to the importance of avoiding discrimination. The concept of 'special contribution' in the context of inherited wealth will also be considered.

---

[3] *Miller v Miller and McFarlane v McFarlane* [2006] UKHL 24 para 12

(g) **The conduct of each party such that it would be inequitable to disregard it.**

While this factor does not have a direct bearing on inherited wealth, it is conceivable that conduct by one party could influence a court's decision as to the extent to which inherited property might be invaded in order to do fairness.

(h) **The value of any benefit that a party will lose the chance of acquiring as a result of the marriage ending.**

The classic example of this relates to pension assets. As a result of no longer being married, benefits such as death in service will no longer be available to a former spouse. The concept may also apply to trust assets where spouses are included within the class of beneficiaries and will no longer be so included upon divorce.

There is no hierarchy of section 25 factors and the list is not exhaustive (the court being required as already noted to have regard to all the circumstances). The consideration of these factors by the court is explored further in the course of this book.

## The Future?

The Divorce (Financial Provision) Bill[4] most recently introduced in the House of Lords by Baroness Shackleton in January 2020 does attempt to introduce greater predictability, defining non-matrimonial property and excluding it from the division of assets on divorce. However it has not progressed and it seems likely to be a long way down the government's list of priorities at present.

---

[4] https://publications.parliament.uk/pa/bills/lbill/58-01/039/5801039.pdf

# CHAPTER TWO
# CASE LAW HISTORY AND DEVELOPMENT

Inherited wealth will often fall to be categorised as non-matrimonial property. This is not a new concept although the terminology has changed over time. The idea that assets which had been brought into the marriage or inherited by one of the parties should be treated differently from the product of the couple's joint endeavours was generally dealt with under s25 of the MCA 1973 Act as one of the circumstances of the case and a contribution by one party to the wealth and well-being of the family. This has been developed and refined over time by the courts.

Before the House of Lords decision in *White v White*[5] in 2000, the established approach was that a wife (for it was usually the woman) should have her "reasonable requirements" met and no more. There was no concept of sharing, and so, in big money cases, this invariably meant the wife received significantly less than 50% of the assets which was also to provide for her income needs. The idea that a wife might have surplus assets to pass to future generations was rejected and this discrimination and patriarchal approach persisted until 20 years ago.

## *White v White*

*White* is a decision of immense importance to family lawyers, marking the end of "reasonable requirements", recognising and denouncing the inherent discrimination that had persisted between the roles of breadwinner and home maker, and introducing the "yardstick of equality" as a cross check for fairness.

In view of that, you might be forgiven for assuming that Mrs White received 50% of the assets. This was after all a marital and business partnership of some 33 years in which both parties had contributed

---
[5] *White v White* [2000] UKHL 54

fully. However in fact she received a share of about one third. The reason for that comes down primarily to inherited wealth.

The facts of *White* were as follows:

The parties married in 1961 when they were both in their mid-twenties. They had three children (all adult by the time of the divorce), one of whom had tragically died. They both came from farming families and throughout the marriage they carried on a dairy farming business. They both contributed cash of a broadly equal amount at the outset. A year after they married they bought their own farm – Blagroves Farm – with a mortgage of £21,000 and Mr White's father had given them about £14k (part gift and part loan) which they grew into their successful farming business. Mr White (senior) later forgave the loan. The farm, which included their home and to which they added further land over time, was held by the two of them jointly. The whole was treated as property of the farming partnership. The value by the end of 1996 was about £3.5m.

The Whites had also farmed another farm – Rexton Farm – as part of their partnership. It had been part of an estate which was owned initially by Mr White's father and was transferred into the joint names of Mr White's father and brothers. This farm was never held in joint names of Mr and Mrs White nor treated as *belonging* to the White's partnership (although they had farmed it). It had a value of about £1.25m. In 1993 Mr White acquired that farm from his father. Shortly after that, in 1994, the marriage broke down.

When the matter came before Holman J at first instance, the total assets were worth about £4.6m. This comprised Mrs White's sole property: £193,300 (mostly pension provision); joint property of £2.67m (including held through the partnership); and Mr White's sole property: £1,783,500 (mostly Rexton Farm).

On the basis of 'reasonable requirements', Holman J ordered that Mrs White receive £800,000 in addition to her own assets. That was enough for a home and Duxbury fund to provide her with an income. Her wish to have enough money to enable her to buy a farm of her own was not considered to be a reasonable requirement.

On appeal the Court of Appeal agreed with Mrs White and awarded her £1.5m which the House of Lords upheld on the husband's further appeal. Mrs White's cross appeal to the House of Lords for an equal share of the assets was also dismissed.

Much can be and has been said about the case from the perspective of equal sharing. Lord Nicholls' seminal judgment confirms the wide powers of the court which should be used to achieve a fair outcome and that in seeking to do so there is no place for discrimination between husband and wife. Therefore the proposed outcome should be checked against the yardstick of equality, this being neither a starting point nor a presumption.

**Their Lordships' Observations on Inherited Wealth**

Lord Nicholls noted that in countries which have a detailed statutory code there is a distinction between inherited property, and property owned before the marriage, on the one hand, and 'matrimonial property' on the other hand. This reflected the widely held view that on the breakdown of a marriage these two classes of property should not necessarily be treated in the same way.

Property acquired before marriage and inherited property acquired during marriage come from a source wholly external to the marriage. Where this property still exists, it is fair for the spouse to whom it was given to be allowed to keep it . The other spouse has a weaker claim to such property than to matrimonial property.

> *"This distinction is a recognition of the view, widely but not universally held, that property owned by one spouse before the marriage, and inherited property whenever acquired, stand on a different footing from what may be loosely called matrimonial property. According to this view, on a breakdown of the marriage these two classes of property should not necessarily be treated in the same way. Property acquired before marriage and inherited property acquired during marriage come from a source wholly external to the marriage. In fairness, where this property still exists, the spouse to whom it was given should be allowed to keep it. Conversely, the other*

> spouse has a weaker claim to such property than he or she may have regarding matrimonial property.
>
> *"Plainly, when present, this factor is one of the circumstances of the case. It represents a contribution made to the welfare of the family by one of the parties to the marriage. The judge should take it into account. He should decide how important it is in the particular case. The nature and value of the property, and the time when and circumstances in which the property was acquired, are among the relevant matters to be considered. However, in the ordinary course, this factor can be expected to carry little weight, if any, in a case where the claimant's financial needs cannot be met without recourse to this property."*[6]

Inherited wealth really came in to the equation in two respects: a) the early loan (subsequently forgiven) from Mr White's father which enabled the young couple to start their business; and b) Rexton Farm which Mr White received from his father shortly before the end of the marriage.

The House of Lords took the view that the early contribution had lost its significance over the 33 year marriage. From the outcome and their comments it is apparent that the inheritance of Rexton Farm carried much more weight, but there was no detailed analysis of to what extent it should be taken into or left out of account.

Lord Nicholls noted that even leaving the inherited Rexton Farm out of account, the first instance judge's decision left Mr White with two thirds of the assets. He noted that *"The initial cash contribution made by Mr White's father in the early days cannot carry much weight 33 years later"*[7] suggesting that the only inherited property that should continue to hold relevance was Rexton Farm. The House of Lords did not increase the Court of Appeal's award to Mrs White of £1.5m out of £4.6m, suggesting that all of its value was excluded from division (although this was not explicit).

---

[6] *White v White* [2000] UKHL 54 para 42-43

[7] Ibid para 45

Lord Cooke clearly had some reservations as to whether the award was quite fair. In his concurring judgment he added:

*"In the present case, bearing in mind that it was a marriage of more than 30 years, that there were three children and that the wife was an active partner in the farming business as well as meeting the responsibilities of wife and mother, the only plausible reason for departing from equality can be the financial help given by the husband's father. I agree, however, that the significance of this is diminished because over a long marriage the parties jointly made the most of that help and because it was apparently intended at least partly for the benefit of both. As Lord Simon of Glaisdale said, in delivering the judgment of the Privy Council in a case under the former New Zealand legislation Dorothy Haldane v George Christopher Haldane [1977] AC 673, 697:*

*'Initially a gift or bequest to one spouse only is likely to fall outside the Act, because the other spouse will have made no contribution to it. But as time goes on, and depending on the nature of the property in question, the other spouse may well have made a direct or indirect contribution to its retention.'*

*"My only doubt is whether the help from the husband's father should be seen as justifying a difference of the order of 20% in the overall shares of the parties. <u>I think that £1.5 million was probably about the minimum that could have been awarded to Mrs White without exposing the award to further increase on further appeal.</u> But I am prepared to accept that the figure was one open to the Court of Appeal in the exercise of their discretion, and that your Lordships should not interfere with it. So I would join in dismissing both appeals."*[8] *(emphasis added)*

Overall White gives us little guidance as to *how much* weight should be given to the inherited nature of assets in each case and *to what extent* inherited assets should be taken into or left out of account, beyond where they are needed. The discretion noted by Lord Cooke is very wide.

---

[8] Ibid para 62-63

What can be taken from the judgment is:

- when present, the factor of an inheritance is one of the circumstances of the case;

- it represents a contribution by one of the parties;

- the judge should take it into account and decide how important it is in the particular case;

- the nature and value of the property and the time that it was acquired are among the relevant matters to be considered;

- however, in the ordinary course, this factor carries little weight, if any, in a case where the claimant's financial needs cannot be met without recourse to the property.

The House of Lords in *White* also briefly touched on the question of a party being able to pass assets on to future generations (see Chapter 11).

### Cases After *White*

Interpretations of Lord Nicholls' judgment followed in the subsequent cases. There was initially debate as to whether he had indicated that inherited property should be ring-fenced or quarantined – effectively exempt from division.

The Court of Appeal in *Cowan v Cowan*[9] seemed to interpret his judgment as meaning that inherited assets should in effect be identified and excluded from the pool of assets to be divided.

Bennett J in *Norris v Norris*[10] rejected that notion. He noted that by statute the court is required to take into account *all* of the property of each party including that acquired during the marriage by gift or succession or as a beneficiary under a trust. Further, such property should not be excluded from the court's discretionary exercise when it comes to division. In this case he noted that the wife could not expect

---

[9] *Cowan v Cowan* [2001] EWCA Civ 679

[10] *Norris v Norris* [2002] EWHC 2996 (Fam)

to be given credit for the contribution she had made through her inherited wealth and then simply have it deducted from her assets before division – that would be tantamount to double counting and mean she "*could have her cake and eat it*"[11]. In reaching his conclusion he referred to the judgment of Nicholson CJ in *Figgins v Figgins*[12] in which the full court of the Family Court of Australia had taken the same view.

Nicholas Mostyn QC (sitting as a deputy High Court judge) in *GW v RW*[13], agreed with Bennett J's approach in this regard and subsequently this has been the general approach – that statute requires the court to have regard to all of the parties' resources. [14]

## *Miller v Miller; McFarlane v McFarlane*[15]

Six years after *White*, the House of Lords hear the joined appeals of *Miller; McFarlane*. The Court acknowledged the need to give further guidance following *White* and their Lordships' words remain central to financial remedy law today, particularly the enunciation of the now established principles of needs, compensation and sharing. We will consider those elements of the case which are relevant to dealing with inherited wealth.

The facts in so far as they are relevant for these purposes, are that *Miller* involved a childless marriage of less than three years' duration where the husband was a successful fund manager. Shortly before the marriage the husband received a payout of £13m net from equity he had received 5 years previously. He invested in shares in a new company called New Star in 2001. The assets were £16.7m when the parties married in July

---

[11] Ibid para 67

[12] *Figgins v Figgins* [2002] Fam CA 688

[13] *GW v RW (Financial Provision: Departure from Equality)* [2003] EWHC 611 (Fam), para [48]–[49]

[14] However, note that Lord Nicholls disagreed with Mr Mostyn QC's statement in *GW v RW* that domestic contributions in a shorter marriage should not give rise to an entitlement to the same proportion of the assets as contributions over a longer marriage – *Miller v Miller and McFarlane v McFarlane* [2006] UKHL 24 paras 18-19.

[15] *Miller v Miller and McFarlane v McFarlane* [2006] UKHL 24

2000, and £17m when they separated in April 2003, plus whatever the husband's shares in New Star were worth (possibly £12m-£18m). The first instance judge had awarded Mrs Miller £5m and this was upheld twice on appeal despite the House of Lords disapproving of the notion that Mrs Miller had a "legitimate expectation" that the marriage would continue.

*McFarlane*, of less relevance for our purposes, concerned the level and term of periodical payments where the available capital was not sufficient to meet need and the wife was entitled to compensation for having compromised her career.

In relation to matrimonial property Lord Nicholls made the following points:

- Matrimonial property constitutes property acquired during the marriage, other than by inheritance or gift to either party; it is the product of the parties' common endeavour i.e. the 'marital acquest'.

- The matrimonial home, regardless of how it was acquired, usually has a central place in a marriage and should normally be treated as matrimonial property.

- Matrimonial property will be subject to the principle of sharing and the yardstick of equality will apply to it, irrespective of the length of the marriage.

- The length of the marriage will be highly relevant where non-matrimonial property is concerned. In a short marriage fairness may require that a party would not be entitled to a share of the other's non-matrimonial property or that there should be a departure from equality. In a long marriage the weight attributed to the contribution represented by non-matrimonial property may sometimes diminish. The weight to be attributed to modest savings brought into a marriage may well be different from the weight to be attached to a valuable heirloom intended to be retained in specie.

# CASE LAW HISTORY AND DEVELOPMENT

- The way the parties organised their financial affairs will also be a factor to take into account.

- He affirmed his words in *White* that non-matrimonial is a circumstance of the case, representing a contribution to the welfare of the family. The nature and value of the property and surrounding circumstances are relevant factors to consider. However it will carry little weight if it is required to meet needs.

- It is not necessary in every case to draw a dividing line between matrimonial and non-matrimonial property. Valuations are often a matter of opinion on which experts may differ and costs can become disproportionate. The court may distinguish between types of property with the degree of particularity or generality appropriate in the case and give such weight as it considers just to a party's non-matrimonial property contribution.

In her judgment Baroness Hale made the following points:

- Family assets include the family home and its contents, assets acquired for the use and benefit of the whole family, such as holiday homes, caravans, furniture, insurance policies and family savings, and also family businesses or joint ventures in which both parties work.

- She considered whether business or investment assets generated solely or mainly by the efforts of one party during the marriage might not be viewed as matrimonial property, however this will rarely need to be addressed.

- In the few cases where this consideration will be relevant, the duration of the marriage may justify departure from equality.

- While the source of assets may be taken into account, the importance of this will diminish over time.

Whilst there might arguably be differences between them as to what is matrimonial property, it is uncontroversial that, at least at the point of receipt, inherited wealth will ordinarily be non-matrimonial property.

## Guidance After *Miller*

In *Rossi v Rossi* Nicholas Mostyn QC sitting as a Deputy High Court Judge noted

> *"In all cases now a primary function of the court is to identify the matrimonial and non-matrimonial property. In relation to property owned before the marriage, or acquired during the marriage by inheritance or gift, there is little difficulty in characterising such property as non-matrimonial (provided it is not the former matrimonial home). The non-matrimonial property represents an unmatched contribution made by the party who brings it to the marriage justifying, particularly where the marriage is short, a denial of an entitlement to share equally in it by the other party".* [16]

Here we see the start of the formulaic approach advocated by Mostyn J in later cases. *Rossi* received Court of Appeal approval in *Jones v Jones*[17] where the formulaic approach to identifying and dividing matrimonial property was employed.

In his summary of the post *Miller* position regarding non-matrimonial property Mr Mostyn QC included the following points at paragraph 24:

> 24.1 *The statute requires all the assets to be valued at the date of trial.*
>
> 24.2 *For the purposes of establishing the matrimonial property in respect of which the yardstick of equality will "forcefully" apply, the value of assets brought into the marriage by gift and inheritance (other than the former matrimonial home), together with passive economic growth on those assets, should be excluded as non-matrimonial property.*
>
> 24.5 *... the court should, without great difficulty, be able to separate the matrimonial and non-matrimonial property. The matrimonial property will in all likelihood be divided equally although there may be deviation from equal*

---

[16] *Rossi v Rossi* [2006] EWHC 1482 (fam) para 10

[17] *Jones v Jones* [2011] EWCA Civ 41 [45]

> division (a) if the marriage is short and (b) part of the matrimonial property is "non-business partnership, non-family assets" (or if the matrimonial property is represented by autonomous funds accumulated by dual earners).

24.6 *The non-matrimonial property is not quarantined and excluded from the court's dispositive powers. It represents an unmatched contribution by the party who brings it to the marriage. The court will decide whether it should be shared and if so in what proportions. In so deciding it will have regard to the reality that the longer the marriage the more likely non-matrimonial property will become merged or entangled with matrimonial property. By contrast, in a short marriage case non-matrimonial assets are not likely to be shared unless needs require this.*

Important guidance as to how the court should approach the 'big money' case where the wealth is inherited was later given by Ward LJ in *Robson v Robson*[18]. The facts and particular aspects of *Robson* are considered later in Chapter 3, however Ward LJ's guidance is a helpful summary and warrants being set out in full.

> *"How then does the court approach the "big money" case where the wealth is inherited? At the risk of over-simplification, I would proffer this guidance:*
>
> *(1) Concentrate on s25 of the Matrimonial Causes Act 1973 as amended because this imposes a duty on the court to have regard to all the circumstances of the case, first consideration being given to the welfare while a minor of any child of the family who has not attained the age of 18; and then requires that regard must be had to the specific matters listed in s 25(2). Confusion will be avoided if resort is had to the precise language of the statute, not any judicial gloss placed upon the words, for example by the introduction of 'reasonable requirements' nor, dare I say it, upon need always having to be 'generously interpreted'.*

---

[18] *Robson v Robson* [2010] EWCA Civ 1171

*(2) The statute does not list those factors in any hierarchical order or in order of importance. The weight to be given to each factor depends on the particular facts and circumstances of each case, but where it is relevant that factor (or circumstance of the case) must be placed in the scales and given its due weight.*

*(3) In that way flexibility is built into the exercise of discretion and flexibility is necessary to find the right answer to suit the circumstances of the case.*

*(4) Like every exercise of judicial discretion, the objective must be to reach a just result and justice is attained when the result is fair as between the parties.*

*(5) Need, compensation and sharing will always inform and will usually guide the search for fairness.*

*(6) Since inherited wealth forms part of the property and financial resources which a party has, it must be taken into account pursuant to subs 2(a).*

*(7) But so must the other relevant factors. The fact that wealth is inherited and not earned justifies it being treated differently from wealth accruing as the so-called 'marital acquest' from the joint efforts (often by one in the work place and the other at home). It is not only the source of the wealth which is relevant but the nature of the inheritance. Thus the ancestral castle may (note that I say 'may' not 'must') deserve different treatment from a farm inherited from the party's father who had acquired it in his lifetime, just as a valuable heirloom intended to be retained in specie is of a different character from an inherited portfolio of stocks and shares. The nature and source of the asset may well be a good reason for departing from equality within the sharing principle.*

*(8) The duration of the marriage and the duration of the time the wealth had been enjoyed by the parties will also be relevant. So too their standard of living and the extent to which it has been afforded by and enhanced by drawing down on the added wealth. The way*

*the property was preserved, enhanced or depleted are factors to take into account. Where property is acquired before the marriage or when inherited property is acquired during the marriage, thus coming from a source external to the marriage, then it may be said that the spouse to whom it is given should in fairness be allowed to keep it. On the other hand, the more and the longer that wealth has been enjoyed, the less fair it is that it should be ringfenced and excluded from distribution in such a way as to render it unavailable to meet the claimant's financial needs generated by the relationship.*

*(9) It does not add much to exhort judges to be 'cautious' and not to invade the inherited property 'unnecessarily' for the circumstances of the case may often starkly call for such an approach. The fact is that no formula and no resort to percentages will provide the right answer. Weighing the various factors and striking the balance of fairness is, after all, an art not a science."*[19]

In his concurring judgment Hughes LJ said:

*"That the origin of assets is a relevant factor in no sense means that the approach to inherited assets ought always to be the same. What is fair will depend on all the circumstances; those cannot be exhaustively stated but will often include the nature of the assets, the time of the inheritance, the use made of them by the parties and the needs of the parties at the time of trial."*[20]

We will look at aspects of this guidance in more detail in the context of subsequent cases, but it is interesting to take stock here in 2010 of the court's position in respect of inherited assets. We have a sense of the court's very wide discretion to consider the statutory factors; weigh each of the factors it considers to be relevant (including the source of the assets) on a set of scales the calibration of which could be influenced more or less by any other circumstance(s); and having done so to collate those various weights and stir them together with further flexibility and discretion, informed by needs, compensation and sharing; and then

---

[19] *Robson v Robson* [2010] EWCA Civ 1171 para 43

[20] Ibid para 95

cross check the final product to see if it measures up against the benchmark of fairness. Further, the exact same recipe need not be followed in the same way in future cases where there are inherited assets.

# CHAPTER THREE
# NATURE OF THE PROPERTY

Lord Nicholls referred to the "nature and value"[21] and the "nature and source"[22] of the property as being of relevance to the court's decision. It is not hard to conceive that, in assessing fairness, certain property which has a particular family connection or sentimental attachment might warrant different treatment from pure cash or investments.

In *P v P* Munby J (as he then was) observed:

> "...there is inherited property and inherited property. Sometimes the fact that certain property is inherited will count for very little. On other occasions that fact might be of the greatest significance. Fairness may require quite a different approach if the inheritance is a pecuniary legacy that accrues during the marriage than if the inheritance is a landed estate that has been within one spouse's family for generations and has been brought into the marriage with an expectation that it will be retained in specie for future generations"

The next section looks further at the nature of the inherited property and how this has influenced the court's decision.

## Farms and Estates

Perhaps the first category of assets that come to mind in the context of inherited wealth are farms and landed estates which are typically passed down through generations. Their use as family home and business, together with the fact that such cases are often "cash poor", can bring into play issues of liquidity and income generation to meet needs, as well as questions around the dynastic nature of the assets.

We have considered *White* in some detail in Chapter 2. It is perhaps worth noting the wife's desire to have a farming business of her own after divorce, which she could not achieve on the first instance judge's

---

[21] *White v White* [2000] UKHL 54 [43]

[22] *Miller v Miller and McFarlane v McFarlane* [2006] UKHL 24 [20]

award but would in principle have capital for following the House of Lords' judgment. Clearly this will not be the desired outcome in every case.

*P v P*[23] was a case involving a 19 year marriage with two children who had special needs. The total assets in the case amounted to about £2.5m mainly comprised of a hill farming enterprise and land of which the husband was the fourth generation of farmer. The wife had worked hard on the farm as well as contributing by running the house and looking after the children. It was acknowledged that the farm was the husband's whole life and the wife said she would rather avoid it being sold, however she sought a financial award that would necessitate that – either 40% of the assets (equality discounted to recognise the source of the assets) or £770,000 which was her housing need plus a Duxbury fund.

Munby J considered that the wife's award should be restricted to her needs. He awarded her £575,000 on a clean break basis which was approximately. 25% of the assets.

He made the following points:

- The bulk of the family's assets represented a farm which had been in the husband's family for generations.

- The farm had been brought into the marriage with an expectation that it would be retained in specie.

- Although the farm business had been in joint names, the land had been retained in the husband's sole name.

- The wife's contribution, full as it was and demanding of her time and strength, was to the family income and family life. It was not to the acquisition of the capital assets.

- This approach would meet the wife's reasonable needs; any other approach would compel a sale of the farm, with devastating implications for the husband.

---

[23] *P v P* [2004] EWHC 1364 (Fam)

- To give her more than she reasonably needed for accommodation and income would tip the balance unfairly in her favour and unfairly against the husband.

- It would not be fair to limit the wife's claim to the husband's free capital; in the circumstances, the wife's reasonable needs must be met.

Although there was a sense of Munby J trying to share the pain, the balance of fairness in this case came down in favour of the farm not being sold. However he went on to say:

> *"That said, the reluctance to realise landed property must be kept within limits. After all, there is, sentiment apart, little economic difference between a spouse's inherited wealth tied up in the long-established family company and a spouse's inherited wealth tied up in the long-held family estates."* (emphasis added)

So it is certainly not the case that a farm will always be preserved, or invaded to a lesser extent than other property; as ever each case will need to be assessed on its own facts.

*Robson v Robson*[24] involved a valuable landed estate

Ward LJ said

> *"It is not only the source of the wealth which is relevant, but the nature of the inheritance. Thus the ancestral castle may (note that I say may not must) deserve different treatment from a farm inherited from the party's father who had acquired it in his lifetime, just as a valuable heirloom intended to be retained in specie is of a different character from an inherited portfolio of stocks and shares. The nature and source of the asset may well be a good reason for departing from equality within the sharing principle."*

In *Robson* the husband was 66 and the wife 54. It was a marriage of 21 years with 2 children aged 20 and 17. The family had been living a

---

[24] *Robson v Robson* [2010] EWCA Civ 1171

lifestyle that was exhausting capital, and which could not have been funded by their income.

The wife's resources, at the trial, were valued at £343,500. The husband's capital resources were valued at £22.3m, including a Scottish estate and an Oxfordshire stately hall and estate worth c. £16m which had been mostly inherited by the husband by the start of the marriage. The husband's father had purchased the estate in 1954 and the husband had lived on the estate ever since.

When they married, the husband and wife lived in a large property on the estate, later moving into the Hall itself. After the marriage broke down the wife moved into another substantial property on the estate.

Valuing property of this nature is often not straightforward as it will depend on many factors including whether it is sold as a whole or split into various lots. In *Robson* matters were further complicated by part of the wider estate being held by a Bermudan Trust company for the benefit of the settlor's grandchildren (the husband's children and his sisters' children).

The husband argued that his father had sought to create a dynasty based on primogeniture and that he was bound to respect his father's wishes and pass on this inheritance to his children. Charles J rejected this, finding that it was an exaggeration. The judge took the view that that the arrangements made by the husband's father were more designed to be tax-advantageous rather than to establish a dynasty. Further the manner in which the husband had used the inherited wealth did not indicate a priority to preserve it for future generations.

Notwithstanding that, the judge gave the husband the chance to put forward a plan to provide security for periodical payments to the wife, noting that he had given *"the husband this opportunity because in my view there is force in the argument that because of the nature and source of the assets, and my findings in respect of them, it would be fair to base the form and amount of the wife's award on, or consider it by reference to, a financial plan advanced by him that enabled him, or assisted him, to retain his inheritance (or in minimising what he had to sell)."*

## NATURE OF THE PROPERTY

The husband failed to put forward any such plan. The judge concluded that there should be a clean break even if this required the sale of the estate: "*The public and private reasons supporting a clean break exist and it can be funded albeit that this might cause the loss of the estate and/or the Scottish estate to the family*"

The order of Charles J, based on the wife's housing needs plus her income fund, required the husband to pay the wife a lump sum of £8m. He ordered the immediate sale of the Cotswold estate to fund this.

After the judgment had been delivered, but before the order was drawn up, the wife informed the judge that she was now expecting to house herself for £4m, rather than the £5m he had provided for, but he did not alter the lump sum award. The husband appealed. Both parties sought to admit fresh evidence: the wife had in fact spent £4.3m on a home; the husband had received about £14m from the sale of the estate, less than the £16m judge had allowed for and his indebtedness had also increased.

The Court of Appeal found that the judge had failed to have regard to all the relevant facts, in particular the wife's actual housing needs. It was also inconsistent for the judge to criticise both parties for being recklessly wasteful during the marriage, while awarding the wife a sum "*to match the standard of living enjoyed during the marriage*". The wife's housing award was reduced by £700,000 and her budget was reduced by 10%.

The Court of Appeal noted that there is a duty to consider a clean break. In some cases the nature of the inherited wealth, and/or the difficulties or unfairness in requiring an inherited asset to be realised, would make it unjust to order a clean break, but *Robson* was not such a case. The possibility that at some time in the future the wife might re-marry could not justify refusing to order a clean break. The husband had shown himself to be unreliable and given the facts and circumstances of this case, a clean break had been inevitable[25]

---

[25] Ibid at paras [80], [81], [83], [86]

Since the parties had drawn upon capital to support their lifestyle, the husband could not complain that the judge ordered the inherited property to continue to fund the wife's future income needs.

Ward LJ went on to offer guidance as to how the court should approach the 'big money' case where the wealth is inherited (this is set out in Chapter 2 – Guidance After Miller).

**Antiques**

The court has referred in a general sense to family heirlooms and valuable assets passed down in specie through generations when talking about the nature of the assets and how that might influence their decision (see e.g. *Robson* above and *Miller* at paragraph 25). However there is relatively little specific consideration of such assets in the reported cases. As a general rule the courts prefer not to get involved in chattels and if parties cannot agree then they risk the court taking a very broad brush approach which has little regard for sentimentalities.

In *Y v Y*[26] Baron J considered a collection of the husband's family antiques and jewellery. These were worth some £2.2 million net. The judge noted that the husband considered them 'sacrosanct' and was strongly opposed to their sale. However she did not accept that they should be left out of account. She found that with the exception of personal gifts to him and family correspondence, such assets were a resource and could be sold to assist his needs. Whilst acknowledging that they had sentimental value, they also had a real monetary value and were available to cover indebtedness. Accordingly, they should be included in the asset schedule (see further detail on *Y v Y* in Chapter 4 – Needs).

All of the assets owned by the parties, whatever their nature, will need to be accounted for at the first stage of the exercise. It may be necessary to appoint specialist valuers. When it comes to determining how those assets should be treated at the second stage of the process, the court will generally take a pragmatic view. If there are surplus assets then the party for whom they hold sentimental value is likely to be able to keep them, with alternative funds or assets being transferred to the other party as

---

[26] *Y v Y* [2012] EWHC 2063 (Fam)

appropriate. However if assets need to be liquidated to effect a fair overall result then the court will not shy away from that course. That applies with greater force where needs cannot be met without recourse to such assets.

As we saw in *Robson* above, a party with strong feelings about retaining particular assets would be advised to have an alternative plan to present to the court which would avoid the sale or transfer of those assets. This might involve some creativity.

From a practical point of view, care should be taken completing the Form E. Insurance values may not be appropriate to use and if values are uncertain then consideration should be given to whether it is worthwhile getting a valuer to provide values at this early stage (especially if both parties can agree to this course) or whether it would be preferable to wait and to seek a direction for the instruction of a valuer at the First Appointment. There may be a limited pool of specialist valuers. The decision may well depend on whether the items in question and/or their values are likely to be in dispute and/or have an impact on the final outcome.

## Trusts

How trust assets will be dealt with on divorce is a subject too large to cover in detail in this book, however clearly those cases involving significant inherited wealth will often involve trust assets.

The fact that assets are held in trust does not put them beyond the reach of the court and they are not automatically ring fenced. If a trust is found to qualify as a nuptial trust, the court has the power to order a variation of it.[27] The court may find that a trust is not a genuine trust but a "sham", particularly if it has been set up with the intention of putting assets beyond the reach of the other party, and in such circumstances consider the assets as beneficially owned by the offending party.

The court will need to decide whether the trust is a resource available to either of the parties. In assessing this the court will consider the reality

---

[27] Matrimonial Causes Act 1973, s 24(1)(c)

of the ownership and control of the trust assets. In *Charman v Charman* the court stated that the court should pose the question whether the trustees, if asked to do so by the respondent party, would be likely to advance to him or her the whole of the capital immediately or in the foreseeable future?[28]

Where trust assets are available as resources of one of the parties, the question may still remain as to whether they represent non-matrimonial property and therefore whether and to what extent it is fair for an order to be made which would require their division. One question which may arise is whether the trust is "dynastic". In *Charman* the husband had a life interest in the income of a trust and the husband, wife and children were discretionary beneficiaries as to capital. The husband had argued that he had set up the trust to benefit future generations and so the trust assets should not be regarded as his resources. The judge had rejected his argument on the facts in view of: the obvious fiscal purpose behind the trust; the husband's inclusion of himself as a named beneficiary; his power to replace the trustees; the contents of his letters of wishes; the absence of any documentary evidence to support his argument; the inference to be drawn from his attempts to prevent the wife having access to trust documents, and other factors. The Court of Appeal upheld this conclusion.[29]

In *Whaley v Whaley*[30] two trusts which the husband argued were dynastic and should be left out of account were included in the computation of the available assets. The trusts were not set up during the marriage by one of the spouses but by the husband's father before the parties' relationship began with the design of benefiting his sons and, potentially, succeeding generations. Black LJ noted that "dynastic" was not a technical term with its own body of principles and global terms for trusts may be unhelpful – individual trusts vary considerably[31]. There was no *"distinct and different test when determining whether resources from a 'dynastic trust' should be treated as*

---

[28] *Charman v Charman* [2007] EWCA Civ 503

[29] *Ibid* at para 47

[30] *Whaley v Whaley* [2011] EWCA Civ 617

[31] Ibid para 48

*part of the husband's resources."* The question that the court must ask is that set out above in the case of *Charman;* in addition *"the court will have regard to the circumstances of the particular trust – how it came into being, who the beneficiaries are, what duties the trustees have, what other relevant terms there are, how it has been administered in practice and so on".* [32]

One of the first considerations when dealing with trust assets is to ascertain the position in respect of jurisdiction; is the trust is governed by English law, and are both the trustees and the assets in England/Wales, or is there an international dimension? If the latter, there may be difficulties relating to the enforcement of an English order and advice will be required in the relevant jurisdiction. A cost benefit analysis should be undertaken early on as to whether assets would indeed be made available to satisfy an order. It may also prove more difficult to obtain information from trustees based overseas (although this varies considerably between jurisdictions).

Where there are trust assets, and particularly if any claim is made in respect of them, care needs to be taken to ensure that requirements as to service are complied with[33] and the question of joinder to the proceedings of the trustees and other (particularly minor) beneficiaries needs to be considered[34].

**Shares and Investments**

In *K v L*[35] the wife had inherited substantial offshore assets in the form of shares about 13 years before she started cohabiting with the husband. At the beginning of the relationship the wife's shares were worth about £300,000. At the date of separation they were worth about £28m; and by the date of trial, 3 years after the separation, they were worth more than £57m.

---

[32] Ibid para 54

[33] Family Procedure Rules 2010 r9.13

[34] Ibid rr9.26B and 9.11

[35] *K v L (Ancillary Relief: Inherited Wealth)* [2011] EWCA Civ 550

It was a 21 year relationship with 3 children. Neither party had worked and so the inherited wealth represented the entirety of the available assets. Dividends from the shares had funded the family's living expenses but the family spending had been extremely modest in the context of the value of the wife's assets. Apart from selling a small number of shares occasionally, the shares remained entirely ring-fenced during the marriage.

The husband sought an award of £18m. Bodey J at first instance valued the family's total net assets at £57m (after deduction of latent capital gains tax) and awarded the husband £5m on the basis that this, plus the husband's existing capital of £300,000, would meet his needs, generously assessed.

The husband appealed arguing that his contribution had not been given appropriate weight and that insufficient account had been taken of the fact that 'the importance of the source of the assets will diminish over time' as stated by Baroness Hale in *Miller; MacFarlane*. He accepted the award met his needs but argued it was disproportionately low in the context of the wife's wealth.

His appeal was dismissed. A finding that, in addition to the equal contributions made by each party to their home life, the wife had made a financial contribution to the marriage of great importance did not discriminate between the parties in any unacceptable way; on the contrary, it correctly recognised a substantive difference.

Wilson LJ, considered that the importance of the non-matrimonial source of the assets **might** diminish over time in certain situations. This might include where the acquisition of matrimonial property diminished its significance; it had been mixed with matrimonial property so as to indicate an acceptance by the contributor that it should be treated as matrimonial; or it had been invested in the matrimonial home which had been treated as a central item of matrimonial property.[36]

In this case the importance of the source of the parties' entire wealth had not diminished. Further, at all times the assets had been ring-

---

[36] *K v L (Ancillary Relief: Inherited Wealth)* [2011] EWCA Civ 550 para 18

fenced by share certificates in the wife's sole name and left to grow in value by themselves. For more on the issue of passive growth see Chapter 6.

One might have thought that the nature of the assets in *K v L* (being shares which do not have sentimental attachment and which have grown enormously in value during the course of the marriage so do not represent an inherited way of life for the owner) might have suggested they would be more likely to be shared than, for example, a family heirloom or estate. However in the circumstances of the case, the way in which they were treated and used during the marriage was of greater importance. Note the contrast with *Robson* where the parties had lived beyond their means, funding their lifestyle using the inherited money, and also with *NA v MA* below.

**Business Assets**

Inherited business assets are not excluded from the family balance sheet or from division. However there are many factors to take into account and the dynamic nature of the asset requires that the circumstances of the case are considered very carefully. For example one party might have inherited the business and brought it to the marriage but both parties may have contributed to its growth and success in some way during the course of the relationship. It is likely that the income from the business has supported the family. Shares might have been transferred into a spouse's name. How then should the court deal with this? Finding dividing lines and practical solutions may not be straightforward.

The degree to which business assets will be treated as matrimonial property is considered in some detail at Chapter 6.

**The Family Home**

Typically the matrimonial home is considered a matrimonial asset. How to deal with the family home is often a source of argument between separating parties irrespective of the existence of inherited wealth.. One party will often have a strong desire to remain living there, perhaps with the children of the marriage, while the other wants to sell it to realise their investment and move on. Where the family home is itself an inherited asset which might have been the home of one of the parties prior to the marriage, perhaps even during childhood, this brings an additional dimension and tension. Even in high value cases, the home will often represent a significant proportion of the overall assets and it may not be possible to meet both parties' housing needs without recourse to it. The home may be part of a larger entity such as a farm or landed estate as considered above, and not easily divisible.

Lord Nicholls in *Miller* when considering what would be categorised as matrimonial property said that the family home will be seen as a matrimonial asset, even if it was purchased using non-matrimonial money. This would therefore give each party the same entitlement to a share in it irrespective of the length of the marriage.

> *"The parties' matrimonial home, even if this was brought into the marriage at the outset by one of the parties, usually has a central place in any marriage. So it should normally be treated as matrimonial property for this purpose. As already noted, in principle the entitlement of each party to a share of the matrimonial property is the same however long or short the marriage may have been."* [37]

Lady Hale in her judgment in *Miller* observed that

> *"Family assets were described by Lord Denning in the landmark case of Wachtel v Wachtel [1973] Fam 72, at 90:*
>
>> *"It refers to those things which are acquired by one or other or both of the parties, with the intention that there should be continuing provision for them and their children during their joint lives, and used for the benefit of the family as a whole.""* [38]

She continued:

> *"Prime examples of family assets of a capital nature were the family home and its contents, while the parties' earning capacities were assets of a revenue nature. But also included are other assets which were obviously acquired for the use and benefit of the whole family, such as holiday homes, caravans, furniture, insurance policies and other*

---

[37] *Miller v Miller and McFarlane v McFarlane* [2006] UKHL 24 [22]

[38] Ibid [149]

*family savings. To this list should clearly be added family businesses or joint ventures in which they both work. It is easy to see such assets as the fruits of the marital partnership. It is also easy to see each party's efforts as making a real contribution to the acquisition of such assets."*[39]

Below are some case examples concerning treatment of the family home.

In *Vaughan v Vaughan*[40] the family home had been bought by the husband mortgage free using an inheritance from his father three years before the marriage. Towards the end of the marriage he placed it into the parties' joint names. The court awarded Mrs Vaughan more than half of the equity in the home to meet her housing needs.

On his appeal to the Court of Appeal the husband argued that the district judge at first instance and the circuit judge who heard the first appeal had overlooked the importance of the source of the asset. Wilson LJ giving the judgment of the Court agreed the *"husband's prior ownership of the home carried somewhat greater significance than either the district or circuit judge appears to have ascribed to it."*[41] However, he concluded that it would not have been appropriate for the circuit judge to reduce the district judge's award to the wife. Although an equality of division would meet the wife's needs, the desirability of a clean break was a good reason for departure from equality. The case is better known for arguments around add-back, and had the husband been represented it may be that there would have been greater emphasis on the source of the assets. However the housing needs of the wife were clearly a central factor.

In *K v L*[42] (considered in more detail under **Shares and Investments** above) the pre-marriage assets of the wife had not been intermingled with the matrimonial assets and had been effectively 'ring-fenced'. Wilson LJ considered that one circumstance in which the classification

---

[39] check

[40] *Vaughan v Vaughan* [2007] EWCA Civ 1085

[41] Ibid at para 49

[42] *K v L (Ancillary Relief: Inherited Wealth)* [2011] EWCA Civ 550

of what would otherwise be non-matrimonial property could change over time was that it is used for the purchase of an asset such as the matrimonial home. Thus non-matrimonial property, for example inherited funds, would become characterised as matrimonial and subject to the sharing principle if used to purchase the family home. In *K v L* this idea had little impact on the overall outcome since, although inherited monies were used to buy the matrimonial home, it was very modest in comparison to the value of the wife's assets.

In *NA v MA*[43] Baron J awarded the wife £9.176m out of assets of approximately £40m, all of which had been inherited by the husband. They represented the husband's share of the proceeds of sale of the husband's father's business.

There was no marital acquest; the assets had diminished substantially over the later years of the marriage due to the husband having invested in unsuccessful business ventures. It was a marriage of 12 years with two young children. The wife had been pressurised to sign a post nuptial agreement limiting her claims after her affair with the husband's best friend was discovered. The judge did not give weight to the agreement in the circumstances.

However she considered the inherited nature of the husband's assets to be of central relevance, leading her to conclude that this was not a case where there should be an equal division of assets. In giving proper weight to the origin of the assets which should not be invaded unnecessarily she also noted that there was little marital property and so the award would have to be made from the husband's inheritance.

She stated that "*The former matrimonial home falls into a somewhat different category position*" from other assets. She quoted Lord Nicholls in *Miller and McFarlane* (see above) about the matrimonial home normally being treated as matrimonial property whatever its provenance, but added:

---

[43] *NA V MA* [2006] EWHC 2900 (fam)

*"I do not take that to mean that the property must be divided equally but its value and the lifestyle that it produced are relevant factors in the court's consideration of fairness."*[44]

The matrimonial home in this case had sold for £8m, and the judge assessed the wife's housing needs at £4m. She took account of the fact that the post nuptial agreement made reference to half of the gross value of the home as well as the lavish lifestyle that the family had enjoyed. The wife was awarded a further sum of £4.5m to provide her with an income and additional funds to pay off her debts.

Mostyn J in *S v AG*[45] referred to *Miller*, *K v L* and *Vaughan* noting that *"even the matrimonial home is not necessarily divided equally under the sharing principle; an unequal division may be justified if unequal contributions to its acquisition can be demonstrated."*

---

[44] Ibid at para 175

[45] *S v AG* [2011] EWHC 2637 (Fam) para 9

# CHAPTER FOUR

# APPLICATION OF NEEDS AND SHARING PRINCIPLES

The three principles introduced by the House of Lords in *Miller* of needs, compensation and sharing should be applied in every case in the quest for fairness. This chapter considers how the court has applied them in the context of inherited wealth.

**Needs**

Pursuant to s25(2)(b) MCA 1973 the court is required to take into account "the financial needs, obligations and responsibilities which each of the parties to the marriage has or is likely to have in the foreseeable future;"

There is a tendency for judges to use a phrase or concept to aid interpretation of the law, only for a subsequent judge to caution against a gloss being placed on the statute.

Ward LJ in *Robson* gave such a warning:

> "...Confusion will be avoided if resort is had to the precise language of the statute, not any judicial gloss placed upon the words, for example by the introduction of 'reasonable requirements' nor, dare I say it, upon need always having to be 'generously interpreted'".[46]

Needs is clearly a major factor in how the court will treat non-matrimonial property. As Lord Nicholls observed in *Miller*, in many cases the search for fairness will start and end here[47]. It will be the

---

[46] *Robson v Robson* [2010] EWCA Civ 1171 para 43

[47] *Miller v Miller and McFarlane v McFarlane* [2006] UKHL 24 para 12

primary reason for an award to be made from non-matrimonial (including inherited) assets.

In *GS v L*[48] following a 10 year marriage with three children the husband sought to ring fence £1.65m of the £4m total assets on the basis of having brought it into the marriage. The wife sought an equal division plus maintenance (capitalised or otherwise). Eleanor King J divided the non-pension assets almost equally giving the wife £1.7m because this was required to meet the needs of the wife and children, but this was to include an investment fund to provide an income for the wife. The judge considered that the wife should have maintenance for about 5 years and this award balanced the meeting of needs with recognition of the husband's contribution of non-matrimonial property and the desirability of a clean break.

In *AR v AR*[49] all of the assets of somewhere between £21m and £24m (save for £1m in the wife's name) belonged to the husband and mostly originated from gift or inheritance to him. They were in large part farming assets which the husband received from his father and added to using further inherited funds. The parties had been married for nearly 20 years and cohabited for about 5 years previous to that and had a child together.

The husband's case was the wife should have her housing and income needs met on a Duxbury basis. The wife argued she had an entitlement based on sharing and should not be confined to Duxbury.

Moylan J, as he then was, found that the bulk of the wealth was clearly non-matrimonial. It was not the product of the parties' endeavours during the marriage. The form of the wealth had changed in some respects, in particular following the realisation by the husband of his interests in the family company; the family had lived in the inherited home and, in part, they had used the invested income generated from the husband's inherited wealth.

However he considered that nothing had happened to the bulk of the wealth which had changed it into matrimonial property or diminished

---

[48] *GS v L* [2011] EWHC 1759 (Fam)

[49] *AR v AR* [2011] EWHC 2717

the weight to be attached to it as a factor. Therefore the court should be guided, he said, by the principle of need. The sharing principle did not justify any additional or enhanced award to the wife.

The length of the marriage, the wife's contributions and the standard of living, were all factors which could be given appropriate and sufficient weight within the principle of need. However this did not mean she should be confined to a Duxbury award. In the context of the substantial family wealth she was entitled to incur additional expenditure and she should have additional funds to give her financial security rather than just a Duxbury fund designed to run out on her death. He said:

> "In assessing the wife's income needs...the analysis, as has been said on many occasions, is a broad one as the court is considering what income it would be fair for the wife to have available to her, in this case, for the next 30 or so years.....in my judgment the court's task when addressing this factor is not to arrive at a mathematically exact calculation of what constitutes an applicant's future income needs. It is to determine the notional annual income which in the circumstances of the case it would be fair for the wife to receive. Further in a case such as the present, in my judgment the wife is entitled to have sufficient resources to enable her to spend money on additional, discretionary items which will vary from year to year and which are not reflected in her annual budget"[50]

He therefore increased the Duxbury sum of £2.5m to £3.2m. Her total award was £4.3 (including her own assets of £1m) which amounted to about 18% to 20% of the total assets.

In *Y v Y*[51] Baron J noted that the court should be slow to invade inherited property which is non-matrimonial and in a special category, however the fact that property is inherited will carry little weight where needs cannot be met without using it. The husband in that case came from an illustrious family with many successful forbears who had accumulated great wealth. He inherited the beneficial interest in an

---

[50] *AR v AR* [2011] EWHC 2717 at 70 and 71

[51] *Y v Y* [2012] EWHC 2063 (Fam)

Oxfordshire country estate a year before the marriage and it was transferred out of trust to him absolutely four years after the marriage. The net value of the estate was just under £23m. It was a 26 year marriage with 5 children and important aspects of the case included:

- The 15 bedroomed mansion house was the matrimonial home for almost the entirety of the marriage; the children were brought up there and it was the heart of the parties' relationship and family life;

- The estate income was used to support the family lifestyle. The capital value of the estate was also used to fund the family via increased borrowing secured on the estate;

- The standard of living during the marriage was extremely high – life on the estate was *"grand, sophisticated and almost unparalleled"*.

- This was a long marriage to which the wife made a full contribution.

Baron J accepted the husband's counsel's submission that *"there is a graduated scale or spectrum of kinds of inherited wealth and circumstances relevant to the question of sharing. Factors relevant to likelihood of sharing might include:-*

i) *the nature of the assets (e.g. land/property, art, antiques, jewellery on the one hand, and cash or realisable securities on the other);*

ii) *whether the inherited assets have been preserved in specie or converted into different assets, realised or even spent;*

iii) *how long they have been 'in the family';*

iv) *the established or accepted intentions of both the previous holders of the assets and the spouse who has inherited them;*

v) *whether they have been 'mingled' (for example by being put into joint names of the spouses, or by being mixed with assets generated during the marriage);*

*vi)*   *the length of the marriage and therefore the period over which they have been 'enjoyed' by the other spouse;*

*vii)*   *whether the other spouse has directly contributed to the improvement or preservation of the inherited wealth."*[52]

The wife was awarded £8.7m (32.5% of the assets) which included some of the inherited wealth. Needs, said Baron J, have to be interpreted and assessed against the background of the family's wealth.

Needs is a flexible concept to be assessed according to all the circumstances – the level of wealth alone is just one factor and not determinative. A clear example of this is *K v L*[53] where the Court of Appeal upheld an award of £5m to the husband where the assets were worth over £57m. The assets were essentially all non-matrimonial comprising a shareholding inherited by the wife 13 years before the marriage. This had been used to fund the family outgoings – neither party worked – but it had been retained separately and not mixed with other family assets. The family had a remarkably modest standard of living – they lived in an unexceptional suburban property and their expenditure was really quite low in the context of the available wealth. The children had attended non-fee-paying schools. On that basis the award met the husband's needs generously assessed despite it being less than 10% of the assets.

Another factor which may have a bearing on how the court interprets needs is the existence of a nuptial agreement. Nuptial agreements are considered in Chapter 11, however it is noted that subject to the usual caveats as to validity and fairness, such agreements may inform the court's assessment of the appropriate level of need in an individual case.

---

[52] Ibid para 28

[53] *K v L* [2011] EWCA Civ 550

## Sharing

Does the sharing principle apply at all to non-matrimonial property?

A possible interpretation of *Miller* is that only matrimonial property is subject to the sharing principle. However subsequent cases indicated that that was not the case. In *Charman v Charman (No 4)*[54] the court considered that the sharing principle "*applies to all the parties' property but to the extent that their property is non-matrimonial, there is likely to be better reason for departure from equality*". It has also been said that the sharing principle applies with less force in respect of non-matrimonial property.

In *AR v AR*[55] Moylan J said that sharing could be applied to non-matrimonial property if justified by the circumstances of the case (although in that case the non-matrimonial assets were not shared and needs was the guiding principle).

In *K v L* Lord Justice Wilson said

> "*...although non-matrimonial property also falls within the sharing principle, equal division is not the ordinary consequence of its application. The consequences of the application to non-matrimonial property of the two other principles of need and of compensation are likely to be very different; but the ordinary consequence of the application to it of the sharing principle is extensive departure from equal division, often (so it would appear) to 100% – zero%.*"[56]

During the hearing the court asked leading counsel to show them a reported decision in which the assets were entirely non-matrimonial and in which the applicant secured an award in excess of his or her needs by reference to the sharing principle. But they couldn't come up with one.

---

[54] *Charman v Charman* (No 4) [2007] EWCA Civ 503 para 66

[55] *AR v AR* [2011] EWHC 2717 (Fam)

[56] *K v L* [2011] EWCA Civ 550

To date, there have been no reported cases to the writer's knowledge in which entirely non-matrimonial property has been divided in accordance with the sharing principle – the guiding principle has been needs (interpreted in accordance with the standard of living during the marriage etc.). In *JL v SL*[57] Mostyn J referred to the chance of such a case arising being "*as rare as a white leopard*".

In *Hart v Hart* Moylan LJ giving the judgment of the Court of Appeal said: "*the sharing principle applies with force to matrimonial property but does not apply, or applies with less force to non-matrimonial property.*"[58] Since it wasn't necessary to decide the issue he noted that "*the question of whether the sharing principle only applies to matrimonial property must await another case*". The latter remark suggests that the question technically remains open.

**Which Comes First and Which Prevails – Needs or Sharing?**

Lord Wilson giving the judgment of the Board of the Privy Council in *Scatliffe v Scatliffe*[59] said

> "*So in an ordinary case the proper approach is to apply the sharing principle to the matrimonial property and then to ask whether …. the result of so doing represents an appropriate overall disposal. In particular it should ask whether the principles of need and/or of compensation, best explained in the speech of Lady Hale in the Miller case at paras 137 to 144, require additional adjustment in the form of transfer to one party of further property, even of non-matrimonial property, held by the other.*"

This would suggest the sharing principle should be addressed first and the outcome should then be checked against needs. This is also the approach suggested by Mostyn J in *N v F*[60] (see Chapter 6 – the

---

[57] *JL v SL (No 2) (Appeal: Non-Matrimonial Property)* [2015] EWHC 360 (Fam) para 22

[58] *Hart v Hart* [2017] EWCA Civ 1306 para 62

[59] *Scatliffe v Scatliffe* [2016] UKPC 36 at para 25

[60] *N v F* [2011] EWHC 586 (Fam)

Formulaic/Mathematical Approach). However in *Miller* Lord Nicholls had stressed the importance of flexibility:

> *"...In big money cases, the capital assets are more than sufficient to meet the parties' financial needs and the need for either party to be compensated when one party's earning capacity has been advantaged at the expense of the other party. In these cases, should the parties' financial needs and the requirements of compensation be met first, and the residue of the assets shared? Or should financial needs and compensation simply be subsumed into the equal division of all the assets?*
>
> *"There can be no invariable rule on this. Much will depend upon the amounts involved. Generally a convenient course might be for the court to consider first the requirements of compensation and then to give effect to the sharing entitlement. If this course is followed provision for the parties' financial needs will be subsumed into the sharing entitlement. But there will be cases where this approach would not achieve a fair outcome overall. In some cases provision for the financial needs may be more fairly assessed first along with compensation and the sharing entitlement applied only to the residue of the assets. Needless to say, it all depends upon the circumstances."*[61]

In *J v J*[62] Moylan J started by assessing needs before considering sharing. He agreed with the Court of Appeal in *Charman* that if the figure produced by a needs calculation is greater than that produced by sharing, needs prevail:

> *"It is clear that, when the result suggested by the needs principle is an award of property greater than the result suggested by the sharing principle, the former result should in principle prevail"*[63]

The Court in *Charman* had gone on to say that:

---

[61] *Miller v Miller and McFarlane v McFarlane* [2006] UKHL 24 paras 28-29

[62] *J v J (Financial Orders: Wife's Long-term Needs)* [2011] EWHC 1010 (Fam)

[63] *Charman v Charman* [2007] EWCA Civ 503 at para 73

> "... It is also clear that, when the result suggested by the needs principle is an award of property less than the result suggested by the sharing principle, the latter result should in principle prevail".[64]

In *Jones v Jones* (considered in detail in Chapter 6) Wilson LJ noted *obiter* that the higher of the award required by sharing or needs should found the ultimate award. However in *Hart v Hart*[65], Moylan LJ decided that the judge had not fallen into error in making a needs based award to the wife even though the outcome of the calculations he carried out on other bases resulted in higher awards (see Chapter 6 – *Hart v Hart*).

---

[64] ibid

[65] *Hart v Hart* [2017] EWCA Civ 1306

# CHAPTER FIVE

# OTHER RELEVANT FACTORS

There are a number of factors which may carry particular weight in cases involving inherited wealth.

**Time**

The point at which the inheritance is received is a relevant fact which runs through the following factors. If an inheritance is received before or early in the marriage, there is a greater chance of it influencing lifestyle and/or being mingled with matrimonial property over time, especially in a long marriage. However if it was received much later in the marriage, perhaps shortly before separation, it will have had less impact on the marital relationship and been less an integral part of the marriage.

It was made clear in *White*[66] that the contribution from the husband's father made very early in the marriage had lost its weight over the long marriage (see Chapter 2). Whilst in *JL v SL*[67] (see below) the inheritance was received towards the end of the marriage and was judged not to have lost its non-matrimonial character despite some of it being transferred to the husband's account.

In *K v L* Wilson LJ opined that the true proposition to be derived from *Miller; McFarlane*, was that the importance of the source of the assets might diminish over time in certain situations. For example:

(a) *Over time matrimonial property of such value has been acquired as to diminish the significance of the initial contribution by one spouse of non-matrimonial property.*

---

[66] *White v White* [2000] UKHL 54

[67] *JL v SL (Financial Orders: Property inherited during marriage)* [2014] EWHC 3658 (Fam) and *JL v SL (No 2) (Financial remedies: rehearing: non-matrimonial property)* [2015] EWHC 360 (Fam)

(b)  Over time the non-matrimonial property initially contributed has been mixed with matrimonial property in circumstances in which the contributor may be said to have accepted that it should be treated as matrimonial property or in which, at any rate, the task of identifying its current value is too difficult.

(c)  The contributor of non-matrimonial property has chosen to invest it in the purchase of a matrimonial home which, although vested in his or her sole name, has – as in most cases one would expect – come over time to be treated by the parties as a central item of matrimonial property."[68]

## Length of the Marriage

As a general rule, in principle, the entitlement of each party to a share of the matrimonial property is the same however long or short the marriage may have been. A short marriage is no less a partnership of equals than a long marriage; therefore when sharing, rather than need, is the overriding principle, you would expect to see an equal division of the matrimonial property. In *Miller; McFarlane*[69] Baroness Hale raised the prospect of there being some cases where it might not be appropriate to share the matrimonial assets equally, with the length of marriage being a major factor. In *Sharp v Sharp*[70] the Court of Appeal confirmed that in the case of dual career, short, childless marriages where the parties are self-sufficient and have maintained separate finances, even assets that would be considered matrimonial may not be subject to equal sharing, but such cases will arise very infrequently.

The position in relation to inherited property is different. In *Miller*, Lord Nicholls noted that "*The matter stands differently regarding property ('non-matrimonial property') the parties bring with them into the marriage or acquire by inheritance or gift during the marriage. Then the duration of the marriage will be highly relevant.*" He went on:

---

[68] *K v L (Ancillary Relief: Inherited Wealth)* [2011] EWCA Civ 550 para 18

[69] *Miller v Miller and McFarlane v McFarlane* [2006] UKHL 24

[70] *Sharp v Sharp* [2017] EWCA Civ 408

*"In the case of a short marriage, fairness may well require that the claimant should not be entitled to a share of the other's non-matrimonial property. The source of the asset may be a good reason for departing from equality. This reflects the instinctive feeling that parties will generally have less call upon each other on the breakdown of a short marriage.*

*"With longer marriages the position is not so straightforward. Non-matrimonial property represents a contribution made to the marriage by one of the parties. Sometimes, as the years pass, the weight fairly to be attributed to this contribution will diminish, sometimes it will not. After many years of marriage the continuing weight to be attributed to modest savings introduced by one party at the outset of the marriage may well be different from the weight attributable to a valuable heirloom intended to be retained in specie. Some of the matters to be taken into account in this regard were mentioned in the above citation from the White case. To this non-exhaustive list should be added, as a relevant matter, the way the parties organised their financial affairs."*[71]

## Mingling and Treatment of Assets

How inherited property is treated within the relationship will be important. In *H v H*[72] Singer J noted

*"In my view, the approach I should take in this case must be to attempt to evaluate the available assets as at the date of the hearing and then to consider their nature and provenance. If they derive from pre-marriage acquisition or gift, or from intra-marriage gift or inheritance, then (subject to needs requirements) fairness may dictate that they should be wholly or partially left out of the dividing exercise. Here too the circumstances may differ widely: <u>there is a world of difference between the approach to be adopted to (for instance) a pre-marriage property which has been the parties' matrimonial home; and a gifted or inherited fund kept separate from and never mingled</u>*

---

[71] *Miller v Miller and McFarlane v McFarlane* [2006] UKHL 24 paras 23 to 25

[72] *H v H (Financial Provision)* [2009] EWHC 494 (Fam) para 78

*with the matrimonial budget; and a gift or inheritance fully deployed and utilised for family purposes and needs."* (emphasis added)

As we've noted, where inherited funds are applied to the purchase of a family home, to invest in other family assets or ventures, or used to support the family, they can become 'intermingled'. Consequently it may be unclear where the inherited assets start and stop, and they may lose, to some greater or lesser extent, their non-matrimonial character.

The concept was expressed as 'mingling' first in the case of *N v F* where Mostyn J said:

> "... the longer the marriage goes on the easier it is to say that by virtue of the mingling of the property with the product of the parties' marital endeavours the supplier of that property has, in effect, agreed to share it with his spouse".[73]

The idea had previously been expressed by that judge as property being *"merged or entangled"* (*Rossi*[74]).

The case of *White* was the classic case of mingling although it was not referred to as such at the time. Despite the clearly non-matrimonial nature of the property provided by the husband's father early in the marriage, it was used by both parties to build a family business over a period of over 30 years – it lost its non-matrimonial character because of the way it was used by the family and mingled with other assets, and the relevance of its source decreased with time.

Mostyn J in *S v AG*[75] (where the wife had won the lottery) described mingling as when assets become *"part of the economic life of the marriage; utilised, converted, sustained and enjoyed during the contribution period"* – words he adopted from the Australian case of *Farmer and Bramley* [2000] FamCA 1615.

As noted by Mostyn J, mingling can signify an agreement to share the assets as well as making it harder to value the non-matrimonial element,

---

[73] *N v F* [2011] EWHC 586 (Fam) para 9

[74] *Rossi v Rossi* [2006] EWHC 1482 (fam) para 10

[75] *S v AG* [2011] EWHC 2637 (Fam) para 8

and so the degree of mingling will impact on the extent to which non-matrimonial property should be excluded from account.

According to Mostyn J mingling will impact on

1. whether the existence of pre-marital property should be reflected at all – in the first step of his *N v F* approach – and then

2. how much of it should be excluded (less if there has been "*much mingling*"[76]).

Of course how mingling can be assessed and compared from one case to another and how its impact should be reflected will be a judgment for the judge in each case and, whilst highly fact dependent, a broad brush approach is likely. In *N v F* itself there was a long marriage where the husband's pre-marital assets of approx. £2m had been "*well and truly mingled with marital funds*" but Mostyn J concluded that it would be wrong and unfair for none of the premarital wealth to be excluded from sharing and he held that £1m of it should be so excluded. This was clearly a broad assessment which Mostyn J stated took into account the wife's needs.

In *AC v DC*[77] Sir Hugh Bennett, having been referred to *N v F*, was satisfied that this was "*a mingling case*". The husband's business established prior to the marriage had directly funded the family's lifestyle and the wealth had been inextricably mingled, however it would still be unfair for none of it to be excluded from sharing. The judge awarded the wife 40% of the overall net assets.

In *JL v SL*[78] Mostyn stressed that some mingling of moneys does not mean that the non-matrimonial source of the funds is no longer a relevant consideration. In that case the wife had inherited £465,000 towards the end of the marriage and she had put £190,000 into the

---

[76] *N v F* [2011] EWHC 586 (Fam) para 14

[77] *AC v DC* [2012] EWHC 2420 (Fam)

[78] *JL v SL (Financial Orders: Property inherited during marriage)* [2014] EWHC 3658 (Fam) and *JL v SL (No 2) (Financial remedies: rehearing: non-matrimonial property)* [2015] EWHC 360 (Fam)

husband's account. The district judge took the view that the funds should be treated as matrimonial property. Disagreeing and allowing the appeal, Mostyn J considered that those funds had not lost their non-matrimonial quality and that should be reflected in an unequal division of the assets.

In a very recent case handed down in February 2021, *WX v HX*[79], Roberts J considered a situation where both parties had brought wealth to the marriage but the husband was financially savvy and had generated considerable wealth during the marriage, actively setting up tax efficient structures including trusts specifically for the benefit of the family. The judge concluded that the way in which the husband had dealt with his resources – those he brought to the marriage and subsequently generated – had been for the support of the family.

The wife had little knowledge or interest in the financial arrangements but she had various trust interests which the husband had managed on her behalf during the marriage. The funds had remained separate from the family finances except that the wife had used some of the income for her and the children. Despite the involvement of the husband in managing the wife's funds which he argued had 'matrimonialised' them, Roberts J found that they remained non-matrimonial assets. It was impossible to say to what extent the husband's management had increased their value. The wife had never been asked to contribute funds towards the family's properties or projects – the husband had funded everything.

There was a significant portion of matrimonial property that had been put into a trust arrangement which put it beyond the reach of the parties for the purposes of benefiting future generations, and this was left out of account. However Roberts J ordered that the remainder of the matrimonial property would be divided equally and the wife's property would remain her own. The outcome therefore left the parties with matrimonial property of about £19.4m each and the wife with an additional £9m of her own monies. In addition, the husband had conceded that the whole of the value of their Oxford estate (over £10m)

---

[79] *WX v HX (Treatment of Matrimonial and Non-Matrimonial Property)* [2021] EWHC 241 (Fam)

should be attributed to him, even though under the existing trust structures he only had a life interest in it.

This is a clear demonstration of how the way assets are treated during the course of a marriage can result in them being considered matrimonial or not. It is arguably an embodiment of the concern expressed by Arden LJ in *Jones* in respect of passive growth – that the consequences would be to reward a spouse who buried their non-matrimonial assets in the ground rather than the spouse who actively managed them. See further below at Chapter 6 – The Formulaic/Mathematical Approach.

## Lifestyle

The case of *Robson*[80] involved a marriage of 21 years with two children. There were total assets of about £22.5m the vast majority of which had been inherited by the husband. The family had been living off capital to a large degree, essentially beyond their means. The husband argued that it was a dynastic intention of his father to pass the wealth to future generations. The judge rejected that and noted that the assets had been poorly managed and the couple had not actively increased the value of the asset base. The judge awarded the wife £8m on the basis that she needed £5m to rehouse. The Court of Appeal reduced this to £7m due to the wife in fact needing less for her housing when it came to it. The facts are set out more fully in Chapter 3.

As well as referring to the nature of the inherited assets as being relevant to the s 25 exercise, Ward LJ noted that the duration of the marriage and the period of time the wealth has been enjoyed by the parties would also be relevant. Also the standard of living and the extent to which it has been funded by drawing down on the inherited wealth. The way the property has been preserved, enhanced or depleted are factors to take into account as well. The more and the longer that wealth has been enjoyed within the marriage, the less fair it is that it should be ring-fenced and excluded from distribution in such a way as to render it unavailable to meet the applicant's financial needs generated by the relationship.

---

[80] *Robson v Robson* [2010] EWCA Civ 1171

The court accepted that there might be cases where the nature of the inherited wealth, or the difficulties or unfairness in realising the inherited assets, would make it unjust to order a clean break. Although that was not however the case here.

The high standard of living was also a significant factor in *NA v MA*[81] (see Chapter 3 – The Family Home).

*Robson* can be contrasted with *K v L*[82] where the parties lived a very modest lifestyle in the context of the value of the wife's assets. The inherited wealth was drawn upon to support the family, but not to live a lavish lifestyle. This clearly informed the husband's needs as assessed by the court (see Chapter 3 for more detail).

---

[81] *NA V MA* [2006] EWHC 2900 (fam)

[82] *K v L* [2011] EWCA Civ 550

# CHAPTER SIX

# VALUING THE MATRIMONIAL ELEMENT OF INHERITED PROPERTY

It has been made very clear that inherited property will not be ring fenced. Therefore its value will need to be included in the assets at the computation stage of the judicial exercise. This will be the current value as at the date of trial.

However we have seen that non-matrimonial property can be 'matrimonialised' and growth on non-matrimonial property during the course of a marriage may be the result of the joint endeavours of the parties and therefore matrimonial. Therefore, given the different treatment which may be afforded to inherited property (see above discussion in Chapter 4 as to the application of the sharing principle to non-matrimonial property), especially where the overall assets are sufficient to meet needs, it will clearly be desirable to ascertain what part of the inherited property, if any, should be treated as matrimonial.

Judicial approaches to this have not been entirely consistent as considered further below.

For various reasons, ascertaining the extent to which inherited property should be considered non-matrimonial might not be straightforward. In the first place, attributing a value to it at the point of receipt (or the point of the marriage/beginning of the relationship) may not be simple if there was no contemporaneous valuation. Assuming the change in value can be worked out, deciding what proportion of that should be classed as non-matrimonial will depend on factors such as when the property was received, whether it has been mingled and the reasons why its value has changed since receipt.

It will also depend on what type of asset we are dealing with as well as other various circumstances. If it is, for instance, a piece of art which has appreciated over time, this will be purely as a result of passive growth – it has not taken any effort on the part of the owner, either individually or as part of a joint endeavour with their spouse. In these cases, there is a stronger argument that the entire current value should be considered non-matrimonial property.

If the property concerned is a business, the increase in value is likely to have been due at least in part to the work put in by the owning party, possibly also their spouse and potentially other individuals as well. The business income and other resources may have been used for the benefit of the family. In these circumstances it is less clear-cut, and it is arguable that at least some of the growth should be classed as matrimonial property because it has been actively generated during the marriage. There is therefore a difference between passive and active growth.

It is quite likely in the case of a business that there will be both passive and active growth.

What if all or much of the hard work was done by the owning party before the marriage, giving the business a "springboard", or latent potential which has come to fruition during the marriage and significantly increased its value as at that later date? The owning party might say that it would not be fair for the other party to benefit from that earlier effort which had no connection to the marriage. In such a case it might be considered fair either to (a) attribute a higher value to the business at the time of the marriage, thus excluding a greater proportion of the asset from division, or alternatively (b) to attribute a smaller amount of the growth to the matrimonial assets. We'll consider how the courts have approached this.

## The Formulaic/Mathematical Approach

In *FZ v SZ*[83] Mostyn J expressed the firm view that non-matrimonial property needed to be identified and quantified in order to *"inform the percentage share"*.

In *N v F* Mostyn J advocated a two stage formulaic approach which required the judge to *"Identify the scale of the non-matrimonial property to be excluded, leaving the matrimonial property alone to be divided in accordance with the equal sharing principle."*[84]

He elaborated on the process at paragraph 14, summarised as follows:

1. Firstly decide whether the existence of non-matrimonial property should be reflected in the order at all – this depends on duration and mingling

2. Then, if it is fair to reflect it, decide how much of the non-matrimonial property should be excluded (Should it be the actual historic sum? Or less, if there has been much mingling? Or more, to reflect a springboard and passive growth?)

3. The remaining matrimonial property should then normally be divided equally

4. There should be a cross check for fairness using the overall percentage technique

5. And this will always be subject to the question of need.

This has been described as the formulaic or mathematical approach.

Mostyn J reinforced his support for this approach in *JL v SL* saying that the *"court should always attempt to determine the partition between matrimonial and non-matrimonial property. Once it has done so the matrimonial property should be divided equally and there should usually be*

---

[83] *FZ v SZ and others (Ancillary Relief: Conduct: Valuations)* [2010] EWHC 1630 (Fam)

[84] *N v F (Financial Orders: Pre-Acquired Wealth)* 2011 2 FLR 533 para 11

*no sharing of the non-matrimonial property."*[85] In that case the wife had inherited £465,000 shortly before separation but had put the money into the husband's name; the judge found that this did not make it matrimonial property.

In *Jones v Jones*[86] the Court of Appeal adopted the formulaic approach to the valuation and division of matrimonial property.

In *Jones*, the parties separated after 10 years of marriage. The main asset was a company founded by the husband 10 years before the marriage which was involved in the oil and gas industry. Before setting up the company the husband had worked in the industry for 19 years. The company was valued at £2m at the time of the marriage and before the hearing (which was four years post separation) it was sold for £25m net. The husband accepted it was worth £12m at the time of separation.

The wife sought a clean break lump sum of £10m, on the basis that this represented 40% of the total assets. The husband was offering the wife half of the net increase in the value of the company shares between the date of marriage and the date of separation, which was about £5m.

On the basis that the total net assets were in the region of £25m, the judge awarded the wife £5.4m, concluding that, given the importance of the husband's personal abilities and experience to the success of the company, 60% of the value of the company at the date of the separation, and also 60% of the net proceeds of the ultimate sale of the company (£15m), represented a non–matrimonial asset belonging to the husband, which should not be shared.

The judge had found that there were springboards in place in the company at two dates – on marriage and on separation. On separation there was a springboard in place that accounted for the uplift in value from £12m (on separation) to £25m on sale. And at the date of marriage the judge found there was also a springboard so that the company should be taken to be worth more than £2m at that time – indeed only a year after the marriage the husband had received an offer

---

[85] *JL v SL (No 2) (Financial remedies: rehearing: non-matrimonial property)* [2015] EWHC 360 (Fam) para 25

[86] *Jones v Jones* [2011] EWCA Civ 41

to purchase the company for between £6m and £7m which supported this assessment.

There was a valuation carried out to provide the value of the company at the date of the marriage – why did the court not simply accept that? In Wilson LJ's lead judgment in the Court of Appeal, he said that generally the court would not adjust a professional valuation of a company at a specific date to account for latent potential or springboard because such a valuation would generally reflect that element. However in rare cases, a particular professional valuation might fail to reflect significant latent potential and then the valuation would be subject to increase by the court. Here the court put a value of £4m rather than £2m on the company at the date of the marriage to account for this. It reached this conclusion on what it admitted was an arbitrary basis.

Endorsing the approach of Nicholas Mostyn QC sitting as a deputy HCJ in *Rossi v Rossi*[87], Wilson LJ considered that even if a company needs active management to succeed it is still necessary to make some allowance for passive economic growth as well.

So what the court did in *Jones* was raise the £2m value of the company to £4m to account for the springboard and then, in order to account for passive growth, it applied an increase of 116% which was the percentage increase in the FTSE All Share Oil and Gas Producers Index between the date of the marriage and the date of the sale. This increased the figure for the value of the company at the date of the marriage to £8.7m.

The court accepted that this was a difficult task. There were arguments over the applicability of the index, and in some cases there will not be any relevant index at all. However despite the difficulty Wilson LJ was clear that a judge should still attempt to carry out this exercise. He also confirmed that this approach should also apply to assets that are inherited or received by way of gift during the course of the marriage, not just those that were pre-owned.

Wilson LJ said the approach should be:

---

[87] *Rossi v Rossi* [2006] EWHC 1482 (fam)

1. First identify the non-matrimonial assets and the matrimonial assets.

2. Then decide on the appropriate division of each. (In this case there was no reason to do anything other than share the matrimonial assets equally, and give the non-matrimonial assets to the person who had brought them into the marriage).

3. Then, crucially, test the result against the percentage division of the total assets for fairness.

This is consistent with the *N v F*[88] approach set out above.

In *Jones* the non-matrimonial element of the assets had increased to about £9m after the allowances made. This left what the court assessed to be matrimonial assets of £16m, to be divided equally.

Cross checking against the overall percentage division, Wilson LJ considered a fair bracket would be 30–36%. An award of £8m (representing 32% of the total) was within that fair bracket.

Wilson LJ noted *obiter* that the higher of the award required by sharing or needs should found the ultimate award (however note the position in *Hart v Hart*[89]) below.

Although they agreed with the outcome in *Jones*, the rest of the Court of Appeal were not entirely comfortable with the reasoning.

Arden LJ was not in favour of the passive growth approach. She felt that a spouse should be entitled to whatever fairly represented the fruits of a non-matrimonial asset – even if that was achieved through activity. She was concerned that if only passive growth was taken into account, the law would reward the spouse who buried their non-matrimonial assets in the ground rather than the spouse who actively managed them.

Then President, Sir Nicholas Wall, candidly admitted himself to be somewhat relieved that the answer reached by Wilson LJ came to something around a third – which felt fair to him.

---

[88] *N v F (Financial Orders: Pre-Acquired Wealth)* 2011 2 FLR 533

[89] *Hart v Hart* [2017] EWCA Civ 1306

In *Hart v Hart*[90] the Court of Appeal concluded that there was no obligation on a judge to follow the formulaic approach (see further below).

**The Impressionistic/Discretionary Approach**

The formulaic/mathematical method is not universally preferred. Mostyn J refers in *N v F* to there being "*two schools of thought*" where there is pre-marital property. The first is the technique of simply adjusting the percentage from 50%. The alternative (and Mostyn J's preferred) technique is to identify the scale of the non-matrimonial property to be excluded, leaving the matrimonial property alone to be divided in accordance with the equal sharing principle.[91]

Moylan LJ took a different approach from Mostyn J while he was in the High Court and has continued to do so since his elevation to the Court of Appeal. However he says this does not amount to there being two schools of thought on the matter. Rather the differences are examples of the same principle being applied, but applied in a different manner depending on the circumstances of the case.[92]

In *J v J* [93] the approach of Moylan J (as he then was) was to *start* by applying the principle of need and *then* to consider sharing (unlike the Mostyn J approach as set out above). The starting point of assessing need does not require a computation of what proportion of the assets are matrimonial. Where the result suggested by needs was greater than that suggested by sharing then, he said, needs should prevail. Moylan J agreed to wait until judgment had been given by the Court of Appeal in *Jones* before giving this judgment. In *J v J* there were total assets of about £8.5m. The husband's wealth originated from a family company, shares in which were held in family trusts. The company was sold and significant sums transferred to the wife whose non-domiciled status made this a tax efficient strategy.

---

[90] *Hart v Hart* [2017] EWCA Civ 1306

[91] *N v F (Financial Orders: Pre-Acquired Wealth)* 2011 2 FLR 533 paras 10 and 11

[92] *Hart v Hart* [2017] EWCA Civ 1306 para 87

[93] *J v J (Financial Orders: Wife's Long-term Needs)* [2011] EWHC 1010 (Fam)

Moylan J assessed the wife's needs at just over £4m, the equivalent of 46% of the available resources. He considered that this award gave proper weight to the standard of living during the marriage, the length of the marriage, the resources available to the parties and their respective contributions including the husband's contribution of a significant element of non-marital wealth. He observed that if he had separately determined what share of the wealth the wife should receive, absent the application of the need principle, her award would be lower than her entitlement as determined by reference to her needs. He declined to follow the cases which suggested that he must determine what the award would be by reference to both principles, because he was satisfied that any award determined by reference to sharing would be lower than that determined on the basis of needs.

In *C v C*[94] (a case in which Mostyn QC represented the wife) the parties were in dispute about exactly when they began cohabiting and the extent of the husband's pre-marital wealth.

Moylan J acknowledged that certain passages from *Miller; McFarlane* might seem to require almost an account of the sources of the family's wealth. However, these must be read in context and applied in the framework of the Matrimonial Causes Act 1973. *"It would, in my view, be a very regrettable step if parties were obliged or even encouraged to conduct a financial account after a long marriage. I do not consider that this can be what the House of Lords intended."*[95]

He considered it would not always be necessary to distinguish matrimonial from non-matrimonial property and that parties should be discouraged from *"rummaging around in the attic"* . He cautioned against the universal adoption of a formulaic approach because it could lead to real injustice. A flexible approach is required to ensure that the court's focus remains on achieving a result which is fair.

He concluded that the wealth owned by the husband prior to the marriage was substantial and justified a departure from equality. It

---

[94] *C v C* [2007] EWHC 2033 (Fam)

[95] Ibid para 4

would be unhelpful to suggest that the assessment of the extent to which such departure is justified can be calculated by reference to any formula or clear mathematics. He awarded the wife 40% of the overall assets considering that to be a fair result.

A few months before *Jones*, the Court of Appeal heard the case of *Robson v Robson*[96] but no reference was made to it in *Jones*. In contrast with *Jones* a somewhat less mathematical approach was taken.

Ward LJ urged a return to the precise wording of the statute and cautioned against judicial gloss. The statute, he reminded us, is flexible in terms of the weight to be given to each factor, taking into account all the facts and circumstances with the objective being to achieve a just result. And *"Need, compensation and sharing will always inform and will usually guide the search for fairness."*[97]

The case of *Robson* involved a marriage of 21 years with two children. There were total assets of about £22.5m the vast majority of which had been inherited by the husband. The wife received £7m. The facts are set out more fully in Chapter 3.

Wall LJ said *"It does not add much to exhort judges to be 'cautious' and not to invade the inherited property 'unnecessarily' for the circumstances of the case may often starkly call for such an approach. <u>The fact is that no formula and no resort to percentages would provide the right answer.</u> Weighing the various factors and striking the balance of fairness is after all <u>an art not a science</u>."*[98] (emphasis added). This sentiment was reinforced by Hughes LJ who said *"That the origin of assets is a relevant factor in no sense means that the approach to inherited assets ought always to be the same."*

Clearly in a case where <u>all</u> the assets are inherited, the court will be concerned with meeting need rather than valuing the non-matrimonial property by the mathematical exercise used in *Jones*, but *Robson* certainly suggests more of a flexible and impressionistic approach as opposed to a scientific or formulaic one.

---

[96] *Robson v Robson* [2010] EWCA Civ 1171

[97] Ibid para 43

[98] Ibid

This approach where the court considers the nature and quality of the non-matrimonial assets and then, in its discretion, gives the applicant such reduced percentage of the total assets as the judge feels makes a fair allowance for the contribution of the non-matrimonial assets, has been described as the "impressionistic" approach in contrast to the formulaic approach.

It was the impressionistic approach that was used in *Robertson v Robertson*[99] in 2016. The husband had founded the online fashion company ASOS two years before he met the wife. ASOS was very successful and it was accepted that before, throughout and since the cohabitation and marriage, the husband had worked very hard and displayed vision and entrepreneurial skill in developing the company. The husband submitted that his ASOS shares (including those he had recently sold to buy property) were non-matrimonial, being the residue of precisely the same shares that he had already owned in ASOS some two or more years before meeting the wife.

The wife took the *Jones* approach saying that the value of the company at the time of the marriage should be taken and passive growth applied to it. The difference between that figure and the current value of the business must represent active growth and therefore be matrimonial assets.

The expert accountant assessed the net value of the shares uprated for passive growth as at the date the parties began to cohabit at about £4.84m. The total of all the parties' net assets at trial was just under £220m. The wife, sought half of that figure less the £4.84m (so just over £107m). The husband proposed that the wife should retain or receive assets to the net value of just £30m.

Holman J found that the *Jones* approach was instinctively unfair to the husband in all the circumstances. He should be given much greater credit for the work he had done before the marriage; although the pre-existing shares and their proceeds couldn't simply be carved out altogether – they had been part of the family economy, drawn upon for the benefit of the family and they had not been ring-fenced.

---

[99] *Robertson v Robertson* [2016] EWHC 613 (Fam)

The judge exercised a broad discretion and considered it fair to treat the pre-existing shares as half matrimonial and half non-matrimonial. The result was that the wife would receive a total of £69.5m which was 31.7% of the assets. The *Jones* approach would have given her 48.9% of the assets. So this case really demonstrates the potential difference in outcomes of the two approaches. However query whether on the *Jones* approach the cross check as to fairness of overall division might have resulted in a revised outcome.

## Hart v Hart

In 2017 Moylan J gave the judgment of the Court of Appeal in *Hart v Hart*[100] which considered how non-matrimonial assets should be dealt with.

One of the issues the trial judge had had to grapple with was the extent of the non- matrimonial property. The husband, a property developer, had owned significant assets prior to the marriage in 1987 but it was unclear what value should be placed upon them. This was not due to the valuation issues considered in *Jones*, but rather that the husband's disclosure was deficient. The wife, an air hostess, had had relatively little before the marriage although she did have a Porsche. At trial there were assets in the parties' names worth £3.9m and trust assets of £5.5m.

HHJ Wildblood at first instance ordered that the wife should receive £3.5m out of the £9.4m on a needs basis. He had calculated what the wife would receive on 4 different bases:

1. Her needs which came to £3.5m

2. What he referred to as "mingled property", giving the wife half of the joint assets, half of her sole name assets, her own non-marital assets, and 25% of the trust funds. This would produce an award of £3.53m.

3. A 'non-matrimonial calculation' whereby the judge removed both parties' non-matrimonial property from the equation, before dividing the remaining figure equally to produce an award to the wife of £3.85m. (The judge felt this was very

---

[100] *Hart v Hart* [2017] EWCA Civ 1306

unreliable because he essentially had to guess what the husband's pre-marital property was worth due to his non-disclosure).

4. A fourth calculation which comprised the assets in the wife's name, half of the assets in joint names, plus a 25% share of the trust funds and that would give the wife an award of £3.94m.

Although it produced the lowest award of the four approaches, the judge felt that the needs figure was the most principled and scientific approach and therefore awarded her £3.4m. The wife appealed.

The Court of Appeal upheld the judge's award holding that it was not necessary to take a formulaic approach when there is matrimonial and non-matrimonial wealth.

This is what the Court of Appeal said about the approach to be taken:

1. Case management

    First there needs to be a case management decision to decide what factual investigation is required. If this enquiry would be expensive or of doubtful utility then the court would be likely to find that this was not proportionate or required for a fair outcome to be achieved. If it considered that some further enquiry was warranted it would be for the court to determine what degree of particularity or generality was required.

2. Evidence

    Secondly, the court stressed that the normal rules of evidence apply, and if necessary the court can draw inferences as to where the line falls between matrimonial and non-matrimonial property. However if it remains unclear and not feasible to establish a clear line, then the court can undertake a broad assessment and leave the specific determination of how the parties' wealth should be divided to the next stage.

3. Division

It is then for the court to decide the division of the assets. Even if the court had determined the extent of what was matrimonial property and what was not, the court still had to exercise its discretion having regard to all the relevant factors in the case.

4. Exercise of discretion

If the court had not been able to make a specific factual demarcation as to what was matrimonial and not, but had found that the parties' wealth included an element of non-matrimonial property, it would have to decide what award of such lesser percentage than 50% made a fair allowance for this. Here the court did not have to apply any particular mathematical or other specific methodology. It had a discretion as to how to arrive at a fair division and could simply apply a broad assessment of the division which would result in overall fairness.

So immediately we see support for the broader impressionistic approach, rather than the strict mathematical justification for an award.

The wife argued that it was the husband's litigation misconduct that had made it impossible to establish the extent of the non-matrimonial property, therefore preventing the judge from carrying out the *Jones v Jones* exercise in her case. However the Court of Appeal did not accept that the court had to undertake a detailed evidential enquiry whenever the issue of non-matrimonial property was raised[101].

Further, deficiencies in the evidence and a party's litigation conduct do not mandate a particular outcome[102]. Even if a party fails to engage at all with the process, a court would still have to make findings on the evidence before it as to the scale of the resources. This is because the

---

[101] *Hart v Hart* [2017] EWCA Civ 1306 para 99

[102] Ibid para 101

judge has to determine that the proposed award is one which the respondent could pay and which is fair.

The wife also argued that the judge's decision to base the award on her needs had been arbitrary and that she would have received a greater award had the judge been properly able to quantify the extent of the non-matrimonial and matrimonial property. The Court of Appeal thought this argument had more force, but it found that the judge had cross checked his award for fairness and had been entitled to reach the conclusion he had.

It could be considered unfair, that a persistently non-disclosing party should effectively be given the benefit of the doubt. Further, restricting the wife in *Hart* to a needs award does not sit easily with the feeling expressed by the Court on various occasions that the higher of the needs or sharing award should be the ultimate result (see Chapter 4).

However the Court of Appeal has made it clear that the investigation into the extent of non-matrimonial property should now be controlled by the court and in the interests of proportionality the Court may take a broad approach based on the available evidence. The strict mathematical formulation is certainly not mandatory and it will be difficult to appeal a decision of a judge who states that they have cross checked their award for fairness.

In *Christoforou* (see below) Moylan J (as he then was) noted "*The court's assessment is broad because the objective is broad fairness, not arithmetical precision, an objective which is also consistent with the delivery of proportionate justice.*"[103] This rather nicely sums up the *Hart* approach.

**Evidence of Non-Matrimonial Property**

A further tension, aligned with the difference between the formulaic and impressionistic approach, has been the onus on the party asserting that non-matrimonial property should be excluded from division to provide documentary evidence of its existence and value.

---

[103] *Christoforou v Christoforou* [2016] EWHC 2988 (Fam) para 4

Mostyn J has emphasised the importance of corroborative contemporaneous documentary evidence being submitted at an early stage of proceedings. In *N v F*, Mostyn J said *"If a party is going to assert the existence of pre-marital assets then it is incumbent on him to prove the same by clear documentary evidence"*.[104]

In the 2016 case of *Christoforou* Moylan J did not disagree entirely with the importance of providing evidence of non-matrimonial property but did not think it would be required in every case

> *"I would not subscribe to the view that documentary evidence is necessary in every such case, if this is what Mostyn J envisaged, because the circumstances may be such that, even in the absence of documentary evidence, the court can and should making a finding as to the existence of non-matrimonial property. However, I agree with the underlying force of his observation, namely that, if a party seeks to establish the existence of non-matrimonial property, this must be demonstrated by clear evidence which does not require the court to engage in the sort of detailed forensic analysis which the husband's case in the present proceedings has required."*[105]

In *Christoforou* there had been a 34 year marriage with two children. Neither party had any significant wealth at the time of the marriage, but the husband had since established a successful property business and there were now total assets of between £50m and £55m. The husband sought a departure from equality asserting that some of the properties were non-marital assets due to significant contributions made by his parents. However Moylan J rejected that any of the properties were sufficiently from a source external to the marriage to justify being classed as non-marital and/or that there were any or sufficient non-marital contributions to justify anything other than equal division. The husband had failed to produce clear evidence in support of his case.

In *Hart* Moylan LJ stressed that the evidence of non-matrimonial property need not be documentary *"I do not agree with Mostyn J's comment in N v F that a party would need to prove the existence of pre-*

---

[104] *N v F* [2011] EWHC 586 (Fam) para 24

[105] *Christoforou v Christoforou* [2016] EWHC 2988 (Fam) para 77

*marital assets 'by clear documentary evidence' (at para [24]). There is no reason to limit the form or scope of the evidence by which the existence of such property can be established. The normal evidential rules apply. These include the court's ability to draw inferences if such are warranted"*[106]

The court is not under an obligation to undertake a detailed evidential enquiry in every case, however it still has to make findings on such evidence as there is, including by drawing such inferences as may be appropriate (adverse or otherwise). Deficiencies in the evidence and/or litigation conduct do not mandate a particular outcome.

**Treatment of Valuation Evidence**

Reference has been made in various cases to expert evidence being a matter of opinion and that experts often differ[107]. The instruction of an expert, particularly a single joint expert as is the court's preferred approach, involves taking a risk that the approach the expert takes and the conclusions they reach do not accord with one or other or both of the parties' views. However the expert report or reports does not necessarily represent the end of the story. The court is not bound to accept the expert's valuation and may come to its own conclusions.

The case of *Martin v Martin*[108] raised questions about investigating the value of non-matrimonial property and the treatment of evidence. The parties had separated after 29 years of marriage and had two adult children. The husband and his friend had started a company eight years before the marriage. He subsequently bought his friend out. An expert had put a value on the company as at the date of the marriage of about £300,000. Uprated for inflation this amounted to £1.6m. The expert put the current value of the company at £185m to £227.5m.

Mostyn J at first instance[109] declined to take the expert's value of the company at the date of marriage. Instead he applied a straight line

---

[106] *Hart v Hart* [2017] EWCA Civ 1306 para 91

[107] E.g. *Miller v Miller and McFarlane v McFarlane* [2006] UKHL 24 para 26

[108] *Martin v Martin* [2018] EWCA Civ 2866

[109] *WM v HM (Financial Remedies: Sharing Principle: Special Contribution)* [2017] EWFC 25

approach, effectively drawing a line graph of the company value from 0 at the date of incorporation to the present time (which he put at £221m) and read off the value at the date of the marriage. This resulted in a higher value being attributed to the company at the date of the marriage than the expert said, and led to an assessment that 80% of the company should be considered matrimonial property (as opposed to over 99% which would have been the case on the expert's figures).

The graph below is taken from the judgment and shows how the judge applied the straight line approach in contrast to other growth trajectories.

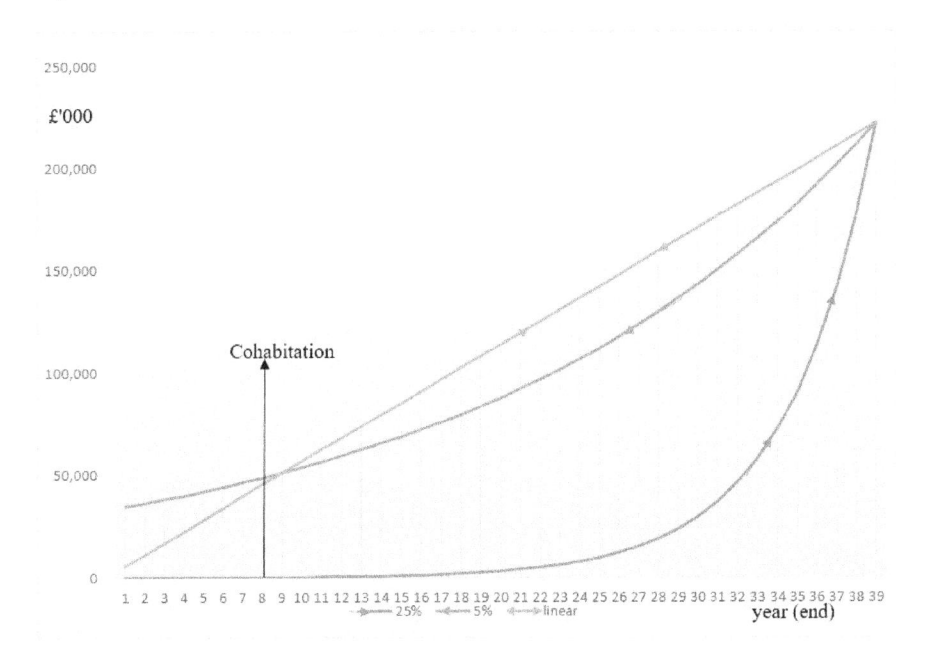

On appeal the Court of Appeal in *Martin* confirmed the *Hart* approach. A judge has an obligation to ensure that the method selected leads to an award which gives *'to the contribution made by one party's non-matrimonial property the weight he considers just... with such generality or particularity as he considers appropriate in the circumstances of the case'*[110]. The judge had been entitled to take the approach he did in seeking to reach a fair result.

---

[110] *Martin v Martin* [2018] EWCA Civ 2866 para 113

So we see that it is down to the judge to be as general or as particular as he or she thinks appropriate in each case and that a quite different approach from that suggested by the valuation evidence could be adopted in the name of fairness.

In *Versteegh v Versteegh*[111], the Court of Appeal upheld the judge's decision to make a *Wells* sharing order which gave the wife a share in the business because he felt he could not make a clear decision about the value of the company. The order gave the wife approximately half the non-business assets (£51.4m) together with a 23.41% interest in a business which had been created by and was run by the husband under a trust structure. Despite such an order being undesirable, King LJ said *"the judge was entitled, and really had no option, but to give weight to the non-matrimonial assets in a more general way as part of the totality of his discretionary exercise."*[112]

It may be a different matter where values are more clearly evidenced. *"In the majority of cases, the court will be able to value the assets, both matrimonial and non-matrimonial, and therefore, if appropriate, make orders by reference to a percentage of the total assets. That is not going to be the case in those less common cases such as the present one, where the court has been unable to place a value on certain of the assets."*[113]

The discretion of the judge in this regard is very wide and it is going to be difficult to appeal decisions on the basis that they have been too formulaic or not formulaic enough, or that the wrong formula has been applied.

There are however certain things that judge carrying out a broad assessment of the evidence needs to do.

In *XW v XH* [114] the wife appealed successfully against a decision of Baker J.

---

[111] *Versteegh v Versteegh* [2018] EWCA Civ 1050

[112] Ibid para 101

[113] Ibid para 99

[114] *XW v XH* [2019] EWCA Civ 2262

The wife had sought a half share in the increase in the value in the husband's shares between the date of marriage and separation based on the expert's valuation. This would give her half of £460m. The first instance judge had awarded her 25% of that sum (£115m) as opposed to the 50% she sought.

The expert had valued the husband's shareholding as at the date of the marriage and had considered whether to apply the concept of a springboard value. He decided that there were arguments for and against this and ultimately did not adjust his valuation to incorporate a springboard or latent potential.

The judge had rejected the judicial approaches in *Robertson*[115] (treating 50% of the value of the business at the date of sale as having been created prior to the marriage) and *WM v HM*[116] (the first instance decision in *Martin* where the straight line approach was used). These would have resulted respectively in 50% or 46.6% of the value of the husband's shares being classified as non-matrimonial property.

Baker J decided that that the evidence did not establish a clear dividing line between matrimonial and non-matrimonial property and it was neither proportionate nor feasible to seek to determine a clear line. On a broad evidential assessment he concluded that there was a significant, though unquantifiable, latent potential in the company at the date of the marriage which was not reflected in the formal valuation.

On appeal Moylan LJ found that the judge had been entitled to undertake a broad evidential assessment and to conclude that the formal valuation did not fully reflect the pre-marital value. He was entitled to apply a springboard despite the expert not having done so. Moylan LJ stressed that the court is undertaking a *retrospective* analysis to determine what part of the *current* value should be treated as marital property, by making "*fair overall allowance*" or by giving the weight the court considers just. Having the benefit of hindsight, the court does not have to take the mathematical route used in *Jones* based on a

---

[115] *Robertson v Robertson* [2016] EWHC 613 (Fam)

[116] *WM v HM (Financial Remedies: Sharing Principle: Special Contribution)* [2017] EWFC 25

prospective valuation as at the date of the marriage – that approach effectively ignores later, known, events. *"The springboard is therefore used as a tool to attribute additional value to non-matrimonial property with the benefit of hindsight in order to achieve a fair result."*

However where Baker J had fallen into error in this case was in failing to set out his determination of the result of his approach and the extent therefore of the marital property. Moylan LJ noted that when he said in *Hart* that in some circumstances the court could undertake a broad evidential assessment, he did not mean that the court did not need to identify how this factor impacted on the award at the quantification stage.

This was particularly problematic because the judge found that there was also a special contribution of the part of the husband (see Chapter 8). Consequently the broad evidential assessment of the judge was not the only factor he applied to determine his award and so the percentage award he decided upon did not speak for itself.

The Court of Appeal decided that it would be fair to both parties to treat as matrimonial property 60% of the share proceeds of just under £490 million, and 40% as non-matrimonial. It rejected the case for a special contribution and therefore shared the matrimonial property of £293m equally between the parties giving the wife £146.5m.

Moylan LJ observed that the approaches in *Robertson* and in *Martin* are examples of the court undertaking the "broad assessment" endorsed by *Hart*[117], and are consistent with the principle that there is no single route to determining what assets are marital.

In the recent case of *WX v HX*, Roberts J summed up the required approach following *Hart* and *XH v XW*:

> *"Thus it is clear that what is required of a financial remedy judgment is sufficient clarity to identify or explain how the court's award has been determined or calculated. The degree to which it will*

---

[117] *Hart v Hart* [2017] EWCA Civ 1306 para 96

*be possible to specify numerically the precise basis of the court's determination will depend upon the nature and quality of the evidence which is available for these purposes."*[118]

In that case the judge observed that much effort (and no doubt money) had been put into trying to demonstrate to what extent the husband's management of the wife's funds had increased the value, and how much the funds would have grown had they simply been left alone. Ultimately the judge found there was insufficient evidence for her to make any sound assumptions and she concluded that the funds remained the wife's non-matrimonial property, having been preserved throughout the marriage as her own separate property.

These cases raise questions about the value of commissioning expensive expert evidence to determine value (particularly of a business) at an earlier date, e.g. the date of the marriage or cohabitation, when the court might decide to apply its own approach, different from that of the expert, in any event. However just because the expert's valuation is not determinative does not mean the report will not be useful to the court in informing its approach and decisions. The court will take account of the evidence available to it and to present no evidence at all as to historic value could be extremely risky. And of course, one does not necessarily know which judge one is going to get.

---

[118] *WX v HX (Treatment of Matrimonial and Non-Matrimonial Property)* [2021] EWHC 241 (Fam)

# CHAPTER SEVEN

# DEPARTING FROM EQUALITY – WHAT IS FAIRNESS?

Having stated that the court will cross check awards for fairness where there is a departure from overall equality as a consequence of non-matrimonial property, what does fairness look like in percentage terms?

In *K v L*[119] Wilson LJ rejected the argument put by the husband's leading counsel that in the reported cases to date the percentage awards had ranged from 23% to 40% where there was non-matrimonial property and therefore the husband's award at first instance of 9.3% (£5.3m out of £57m) was appealable for disproportionality. Wilson LJ noted that the higher awards tended to feature a significant level of matrimonial as well as non-matrimonial property. He distinguished the case of *NA v MA*[120] – the one decision where the award came solely from non-matrimonial property – because the overall assets were lower and the applicant's needs were higher than in *K v L*. There was no reported case known to counsel where the assets were entirely non-matrimonial and in which, by reference to the sharing principle, the applicant secured an award in excess of her or his needs.

Therefore, what is fair in each case will not be governed only by the extent of the departure from equality in percentage terms. The facts of each individual case will need to be assessed carefully and *K v L* was very unusual in the disparity between the size of the assets and the standard of living of the family throughout the marriage. Having said that, Sir Nicholas Wall P expressed his relief in *Jones* that the cross check for fairness revealed a share of something in the region of *"an old-fashioned third"* which had felt instinctively fair to him. It may therefore take very unusual facts for a judge to feel comfortable making a departure to

---

[119] *K v L* [2011] EWCA Civ 550

[120] *NA v MA* [2006] EWHC 2900 (Fam)

below say 25% of the total assets. One reason for this is that there are relatively few cases where the assets are so great that needs interpreted in the context of the available wealth can be met by a lower percentage award.

The cases below involve a significant degree of inherited or otherwise non-matrimonial (eg pre-acquired) assets. They all have their own factual context and varying proportions of matrimonial to non-matrimonial property, so cannot be directly compared, but they simply illustrate the sort of percentage awards that have been made.

| Case | Asset value | Sum Awarded | Percentage award |
| --- | --- | --- | --- |
| NA v MA [2006] | £40m (all inherited) | £9.18m | 23% |
| C v C [2007] | £22.2m | £8.8m | 40% |
| K v L [2010] | £57m (all inherited) | £5m | Less than 10% |
| Robson v Robson [2010] | £22m+ (almost all inherited) | £7m | 32% |
| Jones v Jones [2011] | £25m | £8m | 32% |
| J v J [2011] | £8.5m (almost all inherited) | £4m | 46% |
| AR v AR [2011] | £24m (mostly non-matrimonial) | £4.3m | 18% |
| GS v L [2011] | £4m | £1.7m | 42.5% |
| N v F [2011] | £9.7m (less funds for school fees etc.) | £4.5m | 44.7% |

| | | | |
|---|---|---|---|
| *Y v Y* [2012] | £26.9 almost all inherited | £8.7m | 32.5% |
| *Robertson v Robertson* [2016] | c£220m (half of H's shares deemed to be matrimonial although most of value increase was during marriage) | £69.5m | 31.6% |
| *Hart v Hart* [2017] | £9.4m | £3.5m | 37.2% |
| *Martin v Martin* [2018] | £182m | £72.8m | 40% |
| *Versteegh v Versteegh* [2018] | £102.8m non business assets and business of unknown value | £51.4m – non-business assets (plus interest in business) | 50% of non-business assets plus 23.41% interest in business |
| *XW v XH* [2019] | £530m | £182.5m | 34.5% |

# CHAPTER EIGHT

# SPECIAL CONTRIBUTION

How does the concept of special contribution fit in to inherited wealth cases? *Work v Gray*[121] is the current authority in relation to special contribution. By way of summary, the concept has been confined to reflect a significant, substantive difference in the parties' contributions, which does not require extensive evidential investigation. It is a question of whether there is a disparity in contribution between the parties and whether it is a sufficient disparity to make it inequitable to disregard. It is not that a contribution by one party is unmatched and it will arise only rarely due to the need to avoid discrimination. The contribution will need to be wholly exceptional and deriving from an exceptional and individual quality, however the word "genius" is unhelpful.

In the case of *K v L*[122] Wilson LJ noted that *"the phrase "a special contribution" is now a term of art in the law of ancillary relief which is used to describe a contribution entirely different from that of non-matrimonial property."* It arises when the nature of one spouse's contribution to the creation of matrimonial property demands a departure within the sharing principle from equal division. The Court of Appeal's reference in *Charman* to special contribution being unlikely justify a departure from equality greater that 66.6%–33.3% was in relation to the division of matrimonial property. Therefore the attempt by the husband in *K v L* to suggest that by analogy the wife's non-matrimonial property should not justify a departure of more than one third was rejected.

Special contribution is therefore a separate and distinct concept from the introduction of non-matrimonial property into a relationship.

---

[121] *Work v Gray* [2017] EWCA Civ 270

[122] *K v L* [2011] EWCA Civ 550 para 20

However it is possible to see that the lines may be blurred if growth on non-matrimonial property generates matrimonial property.

In *XW v XH*[123] the husband set up a company some years before the marriage. During the marriage it became hugely successful. From the sale of his shares in 2015/2016 the husband received approximately £370 million and having invested the funds they were worth £490m net by the time of the hearing. The husband had other assets and the wife herself was worth about £34m. The parties had a child who was disabled and for whom the wife was the main carer.

Baker J at first instance made an award to the wife the bulk of which comprised a lump sum of £115 million, being 25% of the growth in value during the marriage of the husband's shareholding, based on the difference between the value at the date of the marriage (per expert evidence) increased by indexation, and the proceeds of sale at about the end of the marriage.

One of the reasons the judge gave for awarding the wife a lower percentage of the growth during the marriage was that the husband's contribution was within the concept of special contribution. The Court of Appeal found that the judge had failed to weigh the wife's contribution in the balance and to consider whether there was such a disparity in the parties' respective contributions that it would be inequitable to disregard. Moylan LJ also observed:

> "I would also add that the issue of special contribution is context specific. As Mr Marks rightly accepted during the course of the hearing, the smaller the amount of the marital wealth the harder it would be for a spouse to rely on it as supporting the conclusion that he or she had made a special contribution. That is why, to repeat, when both these issues are raised, <u>the court needs to state its conclusion as to the extent of the marital wealth to which the issue of special contribution is being applied</u>. For example, in the present case, if the marital wealth was at the level determined by the application of, what I will call, the Martin approach, it would seem significantly

---

[123] *XW v XH* [2019] EWCA Civ 2262

*more difficult for the husband to be able to argue that he had made a special contribution particularly having regard to the judge's determination as to the quality of the wife's contribution".* (emphasis added)

The judge had failed – as noted in Chapter 6 – to assess the amount of marital property as distinct from non-matrimonial and since special contribution could only apply to marital property this was problematic.

It will be rare that special contribution arguments succeed in any event, and therefore it is suggested that it will be extremely unusual that, where an assessment is made that an element of growth on non-matrimonial wealth should be considered marital, the concept of special contribution will have a great deal to add. This is particularly in view of the broad assessment that court is likely to take following *Hart*. Of course it may still be that, separate from the non-matrimonial property, an individual has made a contribution to the matrimonial wealth which could be categorised as special.

# CHAPTER NINE

# FUTURE INHERITANCES

What about assets that a party might inherit at some point in the future – will these be taken into account by a court considering division of resources on divorce? The question may arise and indeed have greater pertinence in relatively modest cases. Where there are already sufficient assets available to meet need, the potential future receipt of non-matrimonial property is likely to be of far less concern to the court. However it may be appropriate to bear it in mind where property currently owned by one spouse's parents could meet a real need.

### The Usual Approach

The courts have been generally unwilling to attach weight to property that a party might inherit at a future date due to the uncertainty about whether, when and in what amount, such expectation will be fulfilled.

An example of this is *J v J*[124] where Moylan J (as he then was) was asked by the wife to take account of the prospect that the husband would receive an inheritance on the death of his parent(s). The husband had defeasible reversionary interests in his father's settlements contingent on the death of both of his parents. Moylan J noted that these were clearly potential resources but, despite taking them into account as potentially available to the husband, they did not have any material effect on his award. *"Having regard to the fact that they are not marital resources, to the ages of the husband's parents and to my assessment of the needs of the parties, these potential resources do not materially affect my application of the principles of need or of sharing."*[125]

---

[124] *J v J* [2011] EWHC 1010 (Fam)

[125] Ibid para 24

In *H v H*[126] the judge at first instance had taken account of the husband's potential inheritance from his mother. On appeal Thorpe J considered that it would be wrong in principle to take account of this hope of succession in anything other than the most general way. It should not be treated as a vested interest likely to fall into possession within the foreseeable future, particularly where the husband's mother was 67 and in good health.

In the case of *HRH Tessy Princess of Luxembourg v HRH Louis Prince of Luxembourg* MacDonald J summarised the current position as follows:

> *"A finding that a party's expectation under a will or other expectation of inheritance constitutes a financial resource will be a rarity by reason of the uncertainties both as to the fact of inheritance and as to the timescales within which the inheritance will be received. These uncertainties will usually make it impossible for the court to conclude that an inheritance is property that is likely to be had in the foreseeable future...."*[127]

In that case the husband's inheritance prospects were not sufficiently certain for them to be considered a financial resource available for distribution. The amount and timing of any inheritance payment was too uncertain for the court to found an award to the wife upon it.

In England and Wales we have testamentary freedom such that an individual can change their will at any time before death, provided they have capacity. This clearly informs the approach of the court adding as it does to the uncertainty of an inheritance materialising. However if there is forced heirship then the position may be slightly different.

---

[126] *H v H* [1993] 2 FLR 335

[127] *Her Royal Highness Tessy Princess of Luxembourg, Princess of Nassau and Princess of Bourbon-Parma v His Royal Highness Louis Xavier Marie Guillaume Prince of Luxembourg, Prince of Nassau and Prince of Bourbon-Parma and another* [2018] EWFC 77 para 76

## Forced Heirship

In *Alireza v Radwan*[128] the Court of Appeal considered a case where the wife's inheritance prospects occurred under Sharia law and therefore were much more certain.

In that case the husband argued that the wife's inheritance prospects under Saudi Arabian 'forced heirship' laws meant she would receive tens of millions of pounds on her father's death and that this was a resource under MCA 1973, s 25(2)(a) such that the wife's financial needs were limited to maintaining and housing her until such time as she remarried or her father died. The trial judge ordered that the wife's needs could be met by her remaining in occupation of the matrimonial home until her remarriage or her father's death (when she would inherit). The Court of Appeal held this to be wrong; the order left the wife with no capital of her own for many years to come and left her future in the hands of a series of men – her husband until the Mesher order was triggered and then either a new husband or her father.

The Court of Appeal endorsed the words of Nourse LJ in *Michael v Michael*[129] where it was held that in the ordinary course of events a party's inheritance prospects are to be disregarded by the court. There were special circumstances where an inheritance is to be considered a financial resource—for example where a person has a terminal illness and it is highly improbable that the testator would revoke the will. It also referred to *C v C*[130] where Munby J held that the husband's vested interest in a property could be considered a financial resource because on the death of his widowed stepmother he would inherit the estate, along with his two siblings, as tenants in common in equal shares. Ordinarily, uncertainties as to the fact of inheritance and when it will occur, will make it impossible to hold that an inheritance prospect is property which is 'likely to be had in the foreseeable future.'

The Court of Appeal in *Alireza* noted that the wife's inheritance prospects due to the concept of 'forced heirship' did not have the same

---

[128] *Alireza v Radwan* [2017] EWCA Civ 1545

[129] *Michael v Michael* [1986] 2 FLR 389

[130] *C v C (ancillary relief trust fund)* [2009] EWHC 1491 (Fam)

uncertainty as a will that was subject to English law and could be a financial resource for the purpose of MCA 1973, s 25(2)(a). The court would be entitled to conclude that the wife would receive a portion of the estate in due course. However that did not necessarily mean that it was appropriate to make an order leaving her ability to meet needs in any way dependent on the prospective inheritance. Here the wife's father's life expectancy was a relevant factor. She was 37 years old with care of three minor children who required a home now, but may well not inherit from her father until she was in her 50s.

### Adjournment

In an extremely unusual situation a court might adjourn an application until the position is more certain. In *MT v MT*[131] in 1992 the wife's application for a lump sum was adjourned until the death of the husband's 83 year old father due to the substantial inheritance that the husband was destined to receive. This was the only way justice could be done, the wife could receive a sum commensurate with her needs and the desired clean break could be achieved. There is a discretionary jurisdiction to order an adjournment but it will be exercised very rarely.

---

[131] *MT v MT* [1992] 1 FLR 362

# CHAPTER TEN

# INHERITANCE AS A BARDER EVENT

Will an inheritance received after a financial order is made have an impact on the settlement?

Finality of legal proceedings is an important aspect of public policy and therefore re-opening of cases and changes to orders will be permitted only in limited circumstances.

In *Critchell v Critchell*[132] the parties reached agreement following an FDR. There were limited assets and the matrimonial home was to be transferred to the wife subject to the mortgage on Mesher terms with the husband having a charge for a sum equal to 45% of the net proceeds of sale of the property. The trigger events were sale, the youngest child reaching the age of 18 or completing secondary education, the wife's death, remarriage or cohabitation for six months.

Less than a month following the order the husband's father died leaving him some money and effectively cancelling a debt which the husband had owed to him. The wife sought leave to appeal the order on *Barder* principles – that the inheritance was an unforeseen event which invalidated the basis or fundamental assumption upon which the consent order had been made. The judge allowed the appeal and varied the order, extinguishing the husband's charge over the property. The husband appealed.

In dismissing his appeal the Court of Appeal noted that the original order had been dictated by need – there was no other way to meet the needs of the wife and children and provide a way for the husband to

---

[132] *Critchell v Critchell* [2015] EWCA Civ 436

repay his debts from the future receipt of funds. Need is a relative concept which is affected by how much there is to go round.

The impact of the inheritance so soon after the order was that the husband no longer needed his interest in the former matrimonial home to repay his debt or discharge his own mortgage. This represented a change in the basis, or fundamental assumption, upon which the consent order had been made. It was not so much that the value of the parties' assets had gone up but rather that there had been a fundamental change in the needs for which provision had to be made.

The Court of Appeal stressed that it was rare for a case to come within the *Barder* principles and it is clear that far from every case where an inheritance is received after an order will meet the criteria. Of course, in order to meet the *Barder* criteria, the event must happen soon after the order and impact the fundamental basis of the order. It is far less likely to apply to inheritances received when the order has not been based firmly on needs. If needs have been met by application of the sharing principle then the inheritance, which represents non-matrimonial property, is unlikely to have such a fundamental impact.

That's not to say that, subject to other circumstances, receipt of an inheritance following a financial remedy order might not justify other applications such as a variation of maintenance or an application for the benefit of a child under Schedule 1 Children Act 1989.

# CHAPTER ELEVEN

# PASSING ASSETS ON

Where matrimonial assets exceed needs and are shared on divorce, each party may have sufficient assets to leave wealth to the next generation (or to such destination as they choose) from their share. If the matrimonial assets do not meet needs and there is recourse to the non-matrimonial, perhaps inherited, assets of one party, can the other party argue that they too should be in a position to pass on assets after their death?

**Will the Court Allow Provision for it in an Award?**

When income needs are capitalised, the Duxbury calculation is generally used to calculate what sum will provide sufficient income for an individual's needs on the basis of their life expectancy – it is designed so that the capital will all be used up at the end of the term. In a number of cases the courts have indicated that where there are sufficient funds available a cushion should be built in to allow for additional expenditure. Is it reasonable to factor in provision for legacies?

In *White* Lord Nicholls considered the wife's wish to be able to leave assets to future generations. This was in the context of a Duxbury award to meet needs for her lifetime. He noted that financial needs are only one of the factors to be taken into account in arriving at the amount of an award.

> *"A parent's wish to leave something to the children would not normally be treated as a financial need, but where resources exceeded needs, that wish could be included as a relevant factor and given appropriate weight.*
>
> *I agree with this proposition to a strictly limited extent. I agree that a parent's wish to be in a position to leave money to his or her children*

*would not normally fall within para (b) as a financial need, either of the husband or of the wife. But this does not mean that this natural parental wish is wholly irrelevant to the s 25 exercise in a case where resources exceed the parties' financial needs. In principle, a wife's wish to have money so that she can pass some on to her children at her discretion is every bit as weighty as a similar wish by a husband."*

*"In my view, in a case where resources exceed needs, the correct approach is as follows. The judge has regard to all the facts of the case and to the overall requirements of fairness. When doing so, the judge is entitled to have in mind the wish of a claimant wife that her award should not be confined to living accommodation and a vanishing fund of capital earmarked for living expenses which would leave nothing for her to pass on. The judge will give to that factor whatever weight, be it much or little or none at all, he considers appropriate in the circumstances of the particular case."*

So unsurprisingly it is once again within the discretion of the judge whether it is appropriate for an applicant to have sufficient provision from non-matrimonial property to be able to leave assets to their descendants, and it will be dependent upon the extent of the resources and the factual context.

In relation to the extent to which a capital award should be amortised to meet income needs (and consequently how much free capital might remain to an individual after the expiration of their life expectancy) see the case of *Waggott v Waggott*[133].

## Lifetime Gifts During the Marriage

Untimely dispositions of assets by one party to their offspring might well be met by avoidance of disposition applications under s37 Matrimonial Causes Act 1973, or arguments for an add back. However the courts will not look upon all gifts to children as improper.

In *F v F*[134] the husband had made gifts totalling over £8m to his four adult children from a previous relationship during the course of the

---

[133] *Waggott v Waggott* [2018] EWCA Civ 727

[134] *F v F (Financial Remedies: Premarital Wealth)* [2012] EWHC 438 (Fam)

marriage. The wife appeared to have raised add back arguments in correspondence but at trial her leading counsel argued rather that the husband should not be able to say the distributions were from premarital wealth and then seek to rely upon the same pre-marital wealth to diminish the wife's fair share of matrimonial assets as that would be double counting. Further that the husband should not be able to argue for making further testamentary dispositions in favour of his elder children.

Macur J considered it was entirely reasonable for the husband to make lifetime bequests to his elder children (regardless of their age) at times when he was also making provision for his younger children and his wife, whether these funds were earned during the course of the marriage or not. The dispositions were indicative of the husband's intent to deal fairly with all of his children during life and after death.

The wife had not proved that the husband had alienated funds with the intention of defeating her claims, and there had been no wanton or reckless behaviour to found an add back argument. These bequests did not adversely impact upon the high standard of marital lifestyle and the wife had not proved that the husband retained any beneficial interest in the assets he had given to his children. The judge therefore rejected the wife's arguments, including that the husband should not be permitted to contemplate further testamentary provision for his children.

# CHAPTER TWELVE

# PROTECTING INHERITED ASSETS – NUPTIAL AGREEMENTS

The subject of pre and post nuptial agreements deserves an entire book. They are considered here specifically in the context of inherited wealth.

Pursuant to the Supreme Court's seminal judgment in *Radmacher*[135],

> *"The court should give effect to a nuptial agreement that is freely entered into by each party with a full appreciation of its implications unless in the circumstances prevailing it would not be fair to hold the parties to their agreement."*[136]

Therefore a court is likely to uphold a nuptial agreement if it was entered into willingly by both parties with a clear understanding of the implications unless, in the circumstances at the time the court is looking at it, it would be unfair. It is therefore usually advisable for there to be full financial disclosure and independent legal advice, although the absence of these things might not themselves be fatal depending on the circumstances of the case. They will be evidence of the parties' understanding of the implications. The agreement must also not be vitiated by fraud or duress.

The Supreme Court noted that the three strands of need, compensation and sharing are relevant to the question of what is fair when a court is considering a case. However the existence and terms of a nuptial agreement is an important factor to be weighed in the balance and capable of altering what is fair.

Specifically in relation to non-matrimonial property the Supreme Court said:

---

[135] *Radmacher (formerly Granatino) v Granatino* [2010] UKSC 42

[136] Ibid paragraph 75

> "*Often parties to a marriage will be motivated in concluding a nuptial agreement by a wish to make provision for existing property owned by one or other, or property that one or other anticipates receiving from a third party. The House of Lords in White v White and Miller v Miller drew a distinction between such property and matrimonial property accumulated in the course of the marriage. That distinction is particularly significant where the parties make express agreement as to the disposal of such property in the event of the termination of the marriage.* **There is nothing inherently unfair in such an agreement** *and there may be good objective justification for it, such as obligations towards existing family members. As Rix LJ put it at para 73*
>
>> *"...if the parties to a prospective marriage have something important to agree with one another, then it is often much better, and more honest, for that agreement to be made at the outset, before the marriage, rather than left to become a source of disappointment or acrimony within marriage.""*

It has since been made very clear by the courts that, subject to the usual and now well-known safeguards, it is a reasonable position for people to take to seek to protect inherited assets in this way. For example see *WW v HW*[137] in 2015. In that case Nicholas Cusworth QC sitting as a Deputy High Court Judge noted that the primary purpose of the agreement was to protect the wife's inherited property from a sharing claim, *"which is an entirely reasonable ambition"*. It was relevant that the husband had been well aware of this purpose and the wife had been clear that she would not marry unless the agreement was entered. The husband had significantly overstated his resources at the time of the agreement to make it appear that he would be able to fall back on his own means and thereby induce the wife to enter the agreement and marry him. In the circumstances of this case it would be fair to hold the husband to his agreement unless, on assessment of his needs (in light of the agreement), a different outcome was dictated.

---

[137] *WW v HW* [2015] EWHC 1844 (fam)

## Needs

The existence of a nuptial agreement will not prevent the court from ensuring needs are met. It is the court and not the parties that decides what provision should be made. The Supreme Court made it plain in *Radmacher* that *"The parties are unlikely to have intended that their ante-nuptial agreement should result, in the event of the marriage breaking up, in one party being left in a predicament of real need, while the other enjoys a sufficiency or more, and such a result is likely to render it unfair to hold the parties to their agreement."*[138]

However a nuptial agreement may affect how needs are assessed. In *WW v HW* Nicholas Cusworth QC said *"The level at which a party's needs should be assessed, if they are not met by an agreement which might otherwise be binding upon them, must surely depend upon all of the circumstances of the case, amongst which the <u>fact of the agreement may feature prominently as a depressing factor</u>. But each case will be different."*[139] (emphasis added

In respect of needs, Mostyn J in *Kremen v Agrest* said that the Supreme Court's decision in *Radmacher* indicated that it is *"likely to be unfair to hold the parties to an agreement which leaves one spouse in a predicament of real need, while the other enjoys a sufficiency or more (para 81). However, need may be interpreted as being that minimum amount required to keep a spouse from destitution. For example, if the claimant spouse had been incapacitated in the course of the marriage, so that he or she was incapable of earning a living, this might well justify, in the interests of fairness, not holding him or her to the full rigours of the ante-nuptial agreement (para 119)*[140].

In *Ipekci v McConnell* Mostyn J further considered the language used by the Supreme Court and felt that it was inappropriate to distinguish the interpretation of need in the context of a nuptial agreement from need in the ordinary sense:

---

[138] *Radmacher (formerly Granatino) v Granatino* [2010] UKSC 42 para 81

[139] *WW v HW* [2015] EWHC 1844 (fam) para 53

[140] *Kremen v Agrest (No.11) (Financial Remedy: Non-Disclosure: Post-Nuptial Agreement)* [2012] EWHC 45 (Fam) para.72 (iv) (c)

> *"I do not take the language used by the Supreme Court, namely "predicament of real need" as signifying that needs when assessed in circumstances where there is a valid prenuptial agreement in play should be markedly less than needs assessed in ordinary circumstances. If you have reasonable needs which you cannot meet from your own resources, then you are in a predicament. Those needs are real needs."*
> [141]

It has been made clear by the Court of Appeal in the case of *Brack v Brack*[142] that, where the parties have contracted out of sharing, the court will usually deal with the case on the basis of needs alone, but the court retains a broad discretion and may make an award in excess of needs if the circumstances of the case require that for fairness to be achieved.

**Meeting the Criteria**

It may seem trite to experienced family practitioners, but if a nuptial agreement is to be used to protect inherited wealth then care should be taken to make sure it meets the well-understood requirements per *Radmacher* and as recommended by the Law Commission's Consultation Paper No 343, Matrimonial Property, Needs and Agreements.

The importance of a nuptial agreement complying with the *Radmacher* criteria was highlighted in *Ipekci v McConnell*[143]. The wife was the great granddaughter of the founder of Avon Cosmetics and was the beneficiary of a number of trusts in the USA with a total value of $65m. The husband was a hotel concierge. The prenuptial agreement they entered into professed to be governed by the law of New York, but was deficient in a number of respects:

- It did not in fact comply with New York law as it did not have the required certification and so would not have been upheld there according to expert evidence;

---

[141] *Ipekci v McConnell* [2019] EWFC 19 para 27 iv)

[142] *Brack v Brack* [2018] EWCA Civ 2862

[143] *Ipekci v McConnell* [2019] EWFC 19

- the legal advice the husband received at the time was not independent as the solicitor in question had previously acted for the wife, and he was not qualified to advise on the law of New York; and

- the agreement did not meet the husband's needs at all.

The judge took account of the fact that all of the wealth had been accumulated from sources external to the marriage so this was not a case for an equal division. The parties had had a reasonably high standard of living during the marriage but due to the way the parties had organised their affairs the husband had made no savings or pension provision for himself. It was in the interests of the children that they could go to stay in a comfortable home with their father and that he was not seen as the poor relation. Accordingly the judge afforded no weight to the agreement. He made a needs-based award in his discretion as he would have done had there been no nuptial agreement at all. Given the complete failure to provide for the husband's needs, the level of the needs-based award was not informed by the agreement. .

The parties' total legal costs were close to £500,000, much of which could potentially have been avoided if the document had been beyond reproach and provided for the husband's needs.

As *Ipekci* shows, an agreement that is totally deficient may not be worth the paper it is written on. Clearly an agreement that ticks all of the *Radmacher*/Law Commission boxes is the preferred situation; however an agreement that is not entirely perfect can still have significant value.

It's clear that if an agreement is not upheld in its entirety, that does not mean that it should be completely ignored. The fact of the agreement and the parties' intentions may still carry weight and influence the ultimate award, so generally speaking some form of agreement will be better than nothing.

As Holman J in *Luckwell v Limata* said:

> "There is no doubt that the decision of the Supreme Court in Granatino v Radmacher [2010] UKSC 42, [2011] 1 AC 534 represented, and now requires, a significant shift in the approach to,

*and weight to be given to, negotiated, drafted and freely signed nuptial agreements of the kinds in the present case when there is no vitiating factor.*

*"I said at the outset of this judgment that the law is not difficult to state. Such agreements must always be given weight, and often decisive weight as part of the circumstances of the case. They may affect not only whether to make any award at all, but also the size and the structure of any award."*[144]

Furthermore, an agreement will record the extent of any non-matrimonial property at the point of marriage and so prove very useful from an evidential point of view, even if the terms are not upheld in their entirety.

It is the very nature of an agreement that both parties sign up to it. If one party refuses to entertain an agreement but the other party who has inherited wealth or stands to inherit still wishes to marry, they would be well advised to keep any inherited assets separate – ringfence them if possible – and avoid mingling or using them to meet family expenditure as far as possible. Certainly they should avoid putting them into the family home or other matrimonial property which is more likely to be subject to the sharing principle if the marriage breaks down.

---

[144] *Luckwell v Limata* [2014] EWHC 502 (Fam) para 129 -130

# CHAPTER THIRTEEN
# THE PRESENT; AND PRACTICAL CONSIDERATIONS

**Where are we now?**

At the end of Chapter 2 we took stock of the position in 2010, when Ward LJ confirmed in *Robson*[145] that the inherited nature of the wealth must be taken into account in the context of all the other circumstances, and that while the factual matrix is relevant, no formula can be applied to determine the outcome; the court has a broad discretion to achieve fairness and the exercise of this is *"an art not a science."* Since then there have been attempts to impose greater structure on the process as advocated by Mostyn J and epitomised by the approach in *Jones*[146], but the impressionistic approach has continued to receive judicial endorsement. Following *Hart*[147] and *XW v XH*[148] it seems it is open to the court to take whatever approach it thinks is most appropriate in the circumstances and to decide upon the degree of *"particularity or generality"* to apply at each stage, picking up on the words of Lord Nicholls in *Miller*[149]. The *Jones* approach is not completely defunct and where there is clear numerical evidence it would be unwise to ignore it as Roberts J's judgment in *WX v HX*[150] indicates. However the Court of Appeal has stressed that the analysis of fairness is retrospective, and the degree to which inherited wealth should be excluded from account should be assessed in light of the circumstances as they now stand. The courts are as keen on proportionality as they

---

[145] *Robson v Robson* [2010] EWCA Civ 1171

[146] *Jones v Jones* [2011] EWCA Civ 41

[147] *Hart v Hart* [2017] EWCA Civ 1306

[148] *XW v XH* [2019] EWCA Civ 2262

[149] *Miller v Miller and McFarlane v McFarlane* [2006] UKHL 24

[150] *WX v HX (Treatment of Matrimonial and Non-Matrimonial Property)* [2021] EWHC 241 (Fam)

have ever been, and careful case management and defining the approach to the evidence at an early stage will be high on the agenda.

**Practical matters**

As with all family finance cases, each case involving inherited wealth must be considered individually on its own facts. Below are some practical considerations and suggestions for the lawyer representing a client in a case where there is inherited wealth.

**Instructions**

Take the clearest instructions possible as to the factual detail and context of the case. Timelines and chronologies will be helpful from the outset and in due course for the court.

**Disclosure**

All of the assets and their current values must be included in the Form E. If accurate values cannot yet be placed on all items, consider whether it is better at this stage to give a broad estimate (clearly marked as such) or to omit values pending a formal valuation.

Bear in mind that instructing a valuer to provide accurate valuations at this point may not be a good use of resources if the other party is going to dispute them. Unless explicitly agreed with the other party in advance, it may be better to wait for a court ordered instruction, perhaps on a joint basis, to avoid duplication. This is especially the case for items where a specialist valuer is required and such experts may be difficult to come by, so instructing too early reduces the choice.

Be clear in the Form E if it is being asserted that particular funds or assets are inherited. The case should be made from the outset and any evidence of the existence and value (including pre-marriage value) of inherited wealth should be collated.

**Case management**

Following disclosure it will be helpful to have a schedule of assets setting out what it is asserted are inherited/non-matrimonial assets and what is matrimonial.

If it is clear that the inherited assets are not going to be left out of account by agreement, perhaps because needs cannot be met without them or there is a dispute as to the extent or (non)-matrimonial nature of them, then careful consideration needs to be given to the management of the case.

Consider if it is going to be of relevance to establish a dividing line between matrimonial and non-matrimonial property. If so, consider carefully whether it is appropriate to instruct an expert and if so the remit of their instruction. Given the guidance in *Hart*, early case management decisions about the depth and detail of the expert evidence will need to be sought, and there may need to be some argument at this early stage about the particularity or generality of the investigations and expert evidence required. It might be advisable to seek specific court endorsement of the questions to be put to the expert; so having these ready in advance of the First Appointment if possible may avoid the need for a further hearing, but additional time may need to be built into the hearing to deal with this.

Is there a case for a preliminary issue hearing to establish the extent of matrimonial and non-matrimonial property? The court's wide discretion to apply what degree of particularity or generality it sees fit, its potentially broad approach to the evidence and then to the division of assets, tends to suggest that there might not be a great deal to be gained from a preliminary issue determination. However if the parties are of a mind that the matter can be settled subject to determining a particular value or question of fact then they might consider arbitration of a specific issue, or an early neutral evaluation.

### Advice/expectation management

It will be important to manage client expectations from the outset. Just because wealth has been in the family for generations does not put it beyond the reach of the courts. The lack of a definite formula or mathematical approach and the breadth of the court's discretion can be difficult for some clients to understand. It will also be important to explain that an expert valuation is not the end of the story and that the court can apply a very flexible approach which may depart from any valuation evidence obtained. Demonstrating various different approaches to the client may help to explain a range of possible outcomes – for example if it involves a business, what would happen if the court applied the straight line approach to your case?

**Presentation**

In dealing with cases involving inherited wealth it may be necessary to think more creatively in order to reach a fair result. Especially where the inherited assets would ideally be retained in specie or cannot easily be liquidated or partially liquidated to meet an award, working out how an award to meet needs can be raised will assist the court.

The courts will not shy away from ordering a sale if that is the only solution, but will be conscious of not destroying an income generator if it can be avoided. Consequently it will be beneficial to both parties to consider how needs can be met. While a clean break will be desirable, it may not be possible in these cases where capital cannot be released. There may have to be ongoing maintenance over a significant period and/or staged payments of capital over time. Consulting a financial advisor from an early stage would be wise to look at cash flow modelling on different scenarios.

Tax is also an important consideration. Cases involving inherited wealth can often include tax planning structures and having to make a distribution to a former spouse at a particular time may not have been in the plan. Consequently advice should be taken at an early stage to ensure that court is aware of the tax implications of distributing assets and if it would be more efficient to handle payments in a particular way then details should be set out for clear presentation to the court.

**ADR**

In this era of financial cuts, COVID backlog and increasing pressure on the courts, it may be wise to consider engaging in a private FDR where appropriate judicial time can be devoted to consideration of more detail and a valuable indication obtained.

Arbitration may also offer a useful route as it can be tailored to the exact needs of the case, enables you to choose a specialist arbitrator and set your own timetable. Even if it is not used as the overall determiner of the outcome of the case, it could be used to determine specific preliminary issues around the valuation or handling of inherited assets as mentioned above – to assist in settlement discussions and/or enable the case to proceed in a more streamlined fashion.

**Other matters**

We have seen that inheritance prospects will rarely be taken into account as a resource available to one of the parties and it is extremely unlikely that an award would be made which required a party to rely on the receipt of an inheritance to meet their needs. However each case needs to be considered on its own facts and future inheritances may form part of the relevant factual matrix.

And finally, in seeking to protect inherited wealth, properly executed marital agreements may offer a significant degree of protection, but if that is not possible then individuals might consider how their inherited asset's non-matrimonial quality can be retained.

# MORE BOOKS BY LAW BRIEF PUBLISHING

A selection of our other titles available now:-

| |
|---|
| 'A Practical Guide to Solicitor and Client Costs – 2nd Edition' by Robin Dunne |
| 'Constructive Dismissal – Practice Pointers and Principles' by Benjimin Burgher |
| 'A Practical Guide to Religion and Belief Discrimination Claims in the Workplace' by Kashif Ali |
| 'A Practical Guide to the Law of Medical Treatment Decisions' by Ben Troke |
| 'Fundamental Dishonesty and QOCS in Personal Injury Proceedings: Law and Practice' by Jake Rowley |
| 'A Practical Guide to the Law in Relation to School Exclusions' by Charlotte Hadfield & Alice de Coverley |
| 'A Practical Guide to Divorce for the Silver Separators' by Karin Walker |
| 'The Right to be Forgotten – The Law and Practical Issues' by Melissa Stock |
| 'A Practical Guide to Planning Law and Rights of Way in National Parks, the Broads and AONBs' by James Maurici QC, James Neill et al |
| 'A Practical Guide to Election Law' by Tom Tabori |
| 'A Practical Guide to the Law in Relation to Surrogacy' by Andrew Powell |
| 'A Practical Guide to Claims Arising from Fatal Accidents – 2nd Edition' by James Patience |
| 'A Practical Guide to the Ownership of Employee Inventions – From Entitlement to Compensation' by James Tumbridge & Ashley Roughton |
| 'A Practical Guide to Asbestos Claims' by Jonathan Owen & Gareth McAloon |
| 'A Practical Guide to Stamp Duty Land Tax in England and Northern Ireland' by Suzanne O'Hara |
| 'A Practical Guide to the Law of Farming Partnerships' by Philip Whitcomb |

| |
|---|
| 'Covid-19, Homeworking and the Law – The Essential Guide to Employment and GDPR Issues' by Forbes Solicitors |
| 'Covid-19, Force Majeure and Frustration of Contracts – The Essential Guide' by Keith Markham |
| 'Covid-19 and Criminal Law – The Essential Guide' by Ramya Nagesh |
| 'Covid-19 and Family Law in England and Wales – The Essential Guide' by Safda Mahmood |
| 'A Practical Guide to the Law of Unlawful Eviction and Harassment – 2nd Edition' by Stephanie Lovegrove |
| 'Covid-19, Residential Property, Equity Release and Enfranchisement – The Essential Guide' by Paul Sams and Louise Uphill |
| 'Covid-19, Brexit and the Law of Commercial Leases – The Essential Guide' by Mark Shelton |
| 'A Practical Guide to Costs in Personal Injury Claims – 2nd Edition' by Matthew Hoe |
| 'A Practical Guide to the General Data Protection Regulation (GDPR) – 2nd Edition' by Keith Markham |
| 'Ellis on Credit Hire – Sixth Edition' by Aidan Ellis & Tim Kevan |
| 'A Practical Guide to Working with Litigants in Person and McKenzie Friends in Family Cases' by Stuart Barlow |
| 'Protecting Unregistered Brands: A Practical Guide to the Law of Passing Off' by Lorna Brazell |
| 'A Practical Guide to Secondary Liability and Joint Enterprise Post-Jogee' by Joanne Cecil & James Mehigan |
| 'A Practical Guide to the Pre-Action RTA Claims Protocol for Personal Injury Lawyers' by Antonia Ford |
| 'A Practical Guide to Neighbour Disputes and the Law' by Alexander Walsh |
| 'A Practical Guide to Forfeiture of Leases' by Mark Shelton |
| 'A Practical Guide to Coercive Control for Legal Practitioners and Victims' by Rachel Horman |

| |
|---|
| 'A Practical Guide to Rights Over Airspace and Subsoil' by Daniel Gatty |
| 'Tackling Disclosure in the Criminal Courts – A Practitioner's Guide' by Narita Bahra QC & Don Ramble |
| 'A Practical Guide to the Law of Driverless Cars – Second Edition' by Alex Glassbrook, Emma Northey & Scarlett Milligan |
| 'A Practical Guide to TOLATA Claims' by Greg Williams |
| 'Artificial Intelligence – The Practical Legal Issues' by John Buyers |
| 'A Practical Guide to the Law of Prescription in Scotland' by Andrew Foyle |
| 'A Practical Guide to the Construction and Rectification of Wills and Trust Instruments' by Edward Hewitt |
| 'A Practical Guide to the Law of Bullying and Harassment in the Workplace' by Philip Hyland |
| 'How to Be a Freelance Solicitor: A Practical Guide to the SRA-Regulated Freelance Solicitor Model' by Paul Bennett |
| 'A Practical Guide to Prison Injury Claims' by Malcolm Johnson |
| 'A Practical Guide to the Small Claims Track' by Dominic Bright |
| 'A Practical Guide to Advising Clients at the Police Station' by Colin Stephen McKeown-Beaumont |
| 'A Practical Guide to Antisocial Behaviour Injunctions' by Iain Wightwick |
| 'Practical Mediation: A Guide for Mediators, Advocates, Advisers, Lawyers, and Students in Civil, Commercial, Business, Property, Workplace, and Employment Cases' by Jonathan Dingle with John Sephton |
| 'The Mini-Pupillage Workbook' by David Boyle |
| 'A Practical Guide to Crofting Law' by Brian Inkster |
| 'A Practical Guide to Spousal Maintenance' by Liz Cowell |
| 'A Practical Guide to the Law of Domain Names and Cybersquatting' by Andrew Clemson |
| 'A Practical Guide to the Law of Gender Pay Gap Reporting' by Harini Iyengar |

| |
|---|
| 'A Practical Guide to the Rights of Grandparents in Children Proceedings' by Stuart Barlow |
| 'NHS Whistleblowing and the Law' by Joseph England |
| 'Employment Law and the Gig Economy' by Nigel Mackay & Annie Powell |
| 'A Practical Guide to Noise Induced Hearing Loss (NIHL) Claims' by Andrew Mckie, Ian Skeate, Gareth McAloon |
| 'An Introduction to Beauty Negligence Claims – A Practical Guide for the Personal Injury Practitioner' by Greg Almond |
| 'Intercompany Agreements for Transfer Pricing Compliance' by Paul Sutton |
| 'Zen and the Art of Mediation' by Martin Plowman |
| 'A Practical Guide to the SRA Principles, Individual and Law Firm Codes of Conduct 2019 – What Every Law Firm Needs to Know' by Paul Bennett |
| 'A Practical Guide to Adoption for Family Lawyers' by Graham Pegg |
| 'A Practical Guide to Industrial Disease Claims' by Andrew Mckie & Ian Skeate |
| 'A Practical Guide to Redundancy' by Philip Hyland |
| 'A Practical Guide to Vicarious Liability' by Mariel Irvine |
| 'A Practical Guide to Applications for Landlord's Consent and Variation of Leases' by Mark Shelton |
| 'A Practical Guide to Relief from Sanctions Post-Mitchell and Denton' by Peter Causton |
| 'A Practical Guide to Equity Release for Advisors' by Paul Sams |
| 'A Practical Guide to the Law Relating to Food' by Ian Thomas |
| 'A Practical Guide to Financial Services Claims' by Chris Hegarty |
| 'The Law of Houses in Multiple Occupation: A Practical Guide to HMO Proceedings' by Julian Hunt |
| 'A Practical Guide to Unlawful Eviction and Harassment' by Stephanie Lovegrove |
| 'Occupiers, Highways and Defective Premises Claims: A Practical Guide Post-Jackson – 2nd Edition' by Andrew Mckie |

| |
|---|
| 'A Practical Guide to Financial Ombudsman Service Claims' by Adam Temple & Robert Scrivenor |
| 'A Practical Guide to Advising Schools on Employment Law' by Jonathan Holden |
| 'A Practical Guide to Running Housing Disrepair and Cavity Wall Claims: 2nd Edition' by Andrew Mckie & Ian Skeate |
| 'A Practical Guide to Holiday Sickness Claims – 2nd Edition' by Andrew Mckie & Ian Skeate |
| 'Arguments and Tactics for Personal Injury and Clinical Negligence Claims' by Dorian Williams |
| 'A Practical Guide to Drone Law' by Rufus Ballaster, Andrew Firman, Eleanor Clot |
| 'A Practical Guide to Compliance for Personal Injury Firms Working With Claims Management Companies' by Paul Bennett |
| 'A Practical Guide to Dog Law for Owners and Others' by Andrea Pitt |
| 'RTA Allegations of Fraud in a Post-Jackson Era: The Handbook – 2nd Edition' by Andrew Mckie |
| 'RTA Personal Injury Claims: A Practical Guide Post-Jackson' by Andrew Mckie |
| 'On Experts: CPR35 for Lawyers and Experts' by David Boyle |
| 'An Introduction to Personal Injury Law' by David Boyle |
| 'A Practical Guide to Subtle Brain Injury Claims' by Pankaj Madan |

These books and more are available to order online direct from the publisher at www.lawbriefpublishing.com, where you can also read free sample chapters. For any queries, contact us on 0844 587 2383 or mail@lawbriefpublishing.com.

Our books are also usually in stock at www.amazon.co.uk with free next day delivery for Prime members, and at good legal bookshops such as Wildy & Sons.

We are regularly launching new books in our series of practical day-to-day practitioners' guides. Visit our website and join our free newsletter to be kept informed and to receive special offers, free chapters, etc.

You can also follow us on Twitter at www.twitter.com/lawbriefpub.